THE EXTINGUISHED CANDLE – RE-LIT

The Extinguished Candle – Re-lit

© John Harris Society 2009

Cover photograph © Eric Parsons 2009

First Edition published 2009

Published by:
Palores Publications,
11a Penryn Street, Redruth, Kernow, TR15 2SP, UK.

Designed & Printed by:
The St Ives Printing & Publishing Company,
High Street, St Ives, Cornwall TR26 1RS UK.

ISBN 978 1 906845 03 2

John Harris

CONTENTS

Humorous Pieces

List of Illustrations

Cover illustration – Eric Parsons
Frontispiece

JOHN HARRIS
Cornish Poet, Dolcoath Miner and Lay Preacher
compiled by Elisabeth Rickard

JOHN HARRIS, the eldest of eleven children born to John and Christiana (Kitty) Harris of Six Chimneys, Bolenowe Carn Nr. Camborne Cornwall on 14th October 1820 and baptized at Camborne Church 4th November the same year.

John Harris Senior was a miner and supplemented his wages by farming a smallholding. He worked as a tributer (a miner paid according to the amount he produced).

Education

At first with a Dame Tregona, at Bolenowe, and several others. Lastly a miner called Roberts who met with an accident underground, and lost a leg. Here he improved himself in reading and spelling etc. He also discovered the secret of rhyme and the mystery of writing couplets. He found it impossible to stop writing. Arthur Langford in his book, 'Git up and Go,' points out that the instruction he later received in Troon Wesleyan Sunday School was without doubt the most consistent although limited to Sundays. The Sunday School had a library. Later at the age of sixteen he became a teacher and eventually a Librarian.

Work

At 9 years of age he worked as a ploughboy for a few months, then he was put to work for a Tin Streamer, or Tinner in Forest Moor for 3 old pence a day.

On John's tenth birthday his father took him to Dolcoath Mine, where John was employed dressing the copper ore.

At 13 his father made the ultimate decision to take him underground. John remained working underground until the latter end of 1857, a period of 24 years. Like his father he became a tributer, experiencing the same problems of uncertainty in respect of his earnings. He said, 'Sometimes I had wages to receive at the end of the month and sometimes I had none.'

Through all the hardships and the contrasting beauty around his home on the hilltop, poetry flowed from him.

Self Improvement

On 2nd August 1842, John wrote, 'I resolve this day to devote Mondays and Wednesdays to grammar, Tuesdays to history or such books as I may have from the (Sunday School) library, Thursdays to poetry reading, Friday to composition, Saturdays to miscellaneous works and Sundays to theology . . . and may my literary acquirements be devoted to the honour and glory of God.'

'Capt. Jimmy Thomas threw open his library door to me and the Reverend Hugh Rogers, the Rector of Camborne, lent me Southey's Remains of Henry Kirke White, which I pondered with great avidity and delight.' Later, the Rev G.T. Bull, first incumbent of Treslothan, seeing that John was fond of poetry loaned him a copy of Romeo and Juliet. Additionally the Rev Bull had formed a little select group to read and discuss poetry to which John was invited.

Marriage

John was married at Camborne Church 11th September 1845 to Christiana Jane Rule of Troon. Their first home was a two roomed house in Troon where their first child, a daughter Jane, was born.

For the greater part of the first year of his married life his earnings averaged only 10 pence a day. John said, 'How we contrived to exist on this small pittance without going into debt, I cannot tell; yet so it was.'

Eventually John's fortune changed when a fairly rich lode of ore was revealed by his labours and that of the little band of miners with whom he worked. In a short space of time he was richer by £200. He goes on to say that . . . 'with a portion of this I built a house at Troon Moor by the river, where we lived happily for many years.'

In 1849 daughter Lucretia was born and in 1857 a son James Howard was born. Sadly, Lucretia died in 1855 aged 6 years and 5 months.

Poetry making

From his school days at Forest Gate, or at home by the kitchen fire, or attending to household duties; whether he drove the horse in the plough, or led the cows to watering, or collected sheep from the down, verse making was the object in his life. So it continued underground at Dolcoath, and on the way home to Bolenowe Carn after completing his shift, John was always composing verse.

Publication of works

A poem which John had written entitled 'The First Primrose,' appeared in a magazine and came to the notice of Dr. George Smith of Trevu, Camborne, whereupon John was invited to Trevu. George Smith took considerable interest in John. Following several visits to Trevu, John plucked up courage to tell Dr. Smith that he would like to publish some of his poems but was unsure as to how to proceed. Dr. Smith advised him to copy some of his best poems and promised to pass them to his friends to obtain their opinion. The result being that a collection of blank verse and rhyme called, 'Lays from the Mine, the Moor, and the Mountain,' was published by subscription in 1853 and dedicated to George Smith who had dealt totally with the business aspect of publication on John's behalf. In fact all his books were published by subscription or forward ordering.

Number of books of poems published 16
Plus 'My Autobiography' 1

Total = 17

Move to Falmouth

John and his family moved to Falmouth in the autumn of 1857 where he took up a position as Scripture Reader. Originally they lived in Wellington Terrace, where their second son John Alfred was born in 1859. Around 1862 they moved to Killigrew Street. According to the 1871 census they had moved yet again to what would be their final home at 85, Killigrew Street.

An indication of the extent of the work carried out by John is contained in the report of the Society for 1877.

Visits to families 2,103
Visits to sick 1,905
Cottage meetings conducted 143
Visits to Maria Camilla

Training School 27
Visits to Workhouses 26
Visits to Sailors' Home 122
Visits to Soup Kitchen 11
Tracts distributed 4,282
Exchanges of Town Mission

Library books 700

Paul Newman — 'Meads of Love'

The setting down of new roots heralded a change of society. Harris's Methodism was ecumenical. Old friends such as John Budge had been Quakers and he was well-disposed towards the Society of Friends. Falmouth was a Quaker stronghold.

He visited Penjerrick, the country home of Robert Were Fox, the leading Quaker, where he drank tea poured from a silver teapot, the silver ore being raised from Dolcoath Mine.

On 6th May 1879 John became a Quaker and joined the Society of Friends at Falmouth.

Early in 1879, John was elected a Fellow of the Royal Historical Society.

John Harris died 7th January 1884 and was buried at Treslothan, near Camborne where his little daughter Lucretia had been laid to rest in 1855.

Elisabeth Rickard of Troon. (2008)

ITEMS NOT FOUND
in 'PEEPS AT A POET'

THE first poetical work which I remember to have read, and which fired my young fancy, being then a boy of only about eight or nine years of age, was an old copy of Burns's "Saturday Night," which I found among some old books on a high shelf belonging to my father.

Though it was somewhat difficult to understand its meaning in the Scotch dialect, yet, by repeatedly perusing it, I was enabled to do so, which filled me with much delight. Soon after this I borrowed a copy of Bloomfield's Poems, which to me at that early age was a rich feast. I now began to write my rhymes on scraps of waste paper, often sewing them together in the shape of a book, and illustrating them with rude drawings of my own. To read these boy-bursts in the still summer evenings to a circle of my companions, who stood wondering around me in the green lane or under the spreading trees, was a joy which none but youthful scribblers feel.

Often during my boyhood my father would send me into the fields to dig what he called "the ditch." This was a portion of the green sward, about two feet from the hedge all around the meadow, which I dug up with a long flat hoe. And here I learned to write poetry and some of my early songs. I used to put my scrap of penciled paper upon the grass, a few feet in advance of the broken ground, and then hoe away making my verse at the same time; and, when I came up to the paper write it down, while the lark sang overhead, the hum of myriad insects filled the mountain air.

Go where I might, my paper scrap and pencil were always at hand, and the world was to me a vast theatre of song. These early effusions were treasured up for many years in a spare drawer – scores of them in number – until, soon after my marriage, one cloudy night we heaped them in the chimney of an upstairs apartment, set them on fire, and silently saw them consumed.

I cannot forget when I first read Campbell's "Gertrude of Wyoming." I was then in my teens, with a thirst for poetry, which could not be quenched. I had selected it from the library in the village school, and, pocketing my treasure hastened to a secluded place where I might peruse it in quiet. It was a little fern-covered corner, on the side of a lovely dell. Here I threw myself down and drew the book from my pocket. At my feet a clear stream went wandering on its way; birds sang on the branches of the trees over my head; sweet flowers shed a delicious fragrance around; bees hummed, and butterflies floated among the honeyed cups, while before me, as through a silver vista, rose the sun-lighted hills of the Land's End, and the blue waters of the Atlantic Ocean. On I read, wading deeper and deeper in liquid beauty, bound to the story by a great spell; and when at last I closed the volume, and started up to climb the hill where my parents resided, I felt soul-full with the lore of the Muses.

The first poetic composition which I prepared for the press was a polemical dialogue between a workman and his master. This was written soon after a strike for wages among some of the dissatisfied miners in a portion of my own district. I well remember how the manufacturing of this dialogue hurried sleep from my eyes for a whole night; and when at last it was finished, I copied it upon several sheets of clean white paper, and took it to a printer at Camborne, who, after keeping it a long time, returned it with these ominous words, "I do not think it is worth printing." Imagine my horror on hearing this crushing speech, and the sadness of my soul as I climbed the old mountain to my mother's dwelling. Suffice it to say that I never more indulged in this species of jingling ware.

Among my early jottings I find the following allusion to my native home on Bolenowe Hill:- "Now at this season (March) when the sun streaks the east, and peers above the hill, we know it is time to rise, and so we get out of bed. When he sinks behind the western mountains, and murky twilight wraps the earth in her shroud, we all gather around the fireside, read a chapter of some interesting volume, and retire to rest as peacefully as the dear little redbreast in the bush. In the morning we are sometimes aroused from our slumber by the voice of a boy going to his work in the mine, who, at the corner of our garden, calls to his blithe companions. When we hear his shrill halloo, it is exactly time to get up, and he it is who is our alarum clock. Peace to his memory! May he live honoured and respected by his companions; grow up to be a wise and happy man; and remember in the full blaze of his glory how, when crowing to his comrades in his boyish glee, he aroused a drowsy poet from his golden dreams."

For about twenty years I worked in Dolcoath mine, Cornwall, – nearly all this time beneath the surface; and this completed the period of my mining career. At the age of twenty-five I married. During the first year of my marriage life, working on copper tribute, fortune was against me, as the annexed lines will show, which were written during this time of depression, in a poem headed "Dolcoath:"

> The last eleven months thou'st been too hard –
> Ten pence per day is all I've had of thee,
> And this has caused the silent tears to flow;
> My wife and I have sat beside the hearth,
> And told our sorrowing tale, with none to hear
> But Him who listens to the raven's cry.
> My silent lyre has rusted in my cot,
> Or, if 'twas strung, 'twas strung to notes of woe –
> But I forgive thee for the cruel past:
> Years of my fleet existence are lopped off
> By thy unwieldy hatchet, and I go
> The silent way, whence there is no return.

Soon after this the tide turned, mineral was discovered, and in four or five months I had earned and pocketed more than one hundred pounds. It is pleasant, at this distance, to look back upon those days, when the muse was dear because of the trial-land through which I passed. And now, amid the wonders of a seaport, where for nine years I have been engaged as Bible-reader, I hear the gush of song, and often feel the promptings of the music-spirit as lovingly as in days gone by; sometimes writing my pieces by the fireside, or walking up and down the room, with the ink-horn in my waistcoat pocket.

REVERIE

Thought now is like a bark,
Toss'd where the waves are dark,
Drifting bewilder'd on some nameless clime:
And so I turn my skiff,
And clear this dangerous cliff,
And anchor in the peaceful port of rhyme.

Here soothing sounds delight,
And on my gladden'd sight
Stretch emerald landscapes, sweetly summer'd o'er:
Castle, and old grey tower,
Rude ivy-mantled bower,
And harpers, rush-screen'd, trilling on the moor.

No hours so sweet to me,
With harp upon my knee,
On some smooth moss-bank, circled round with fays:
Or be it wild with broom,
Or still with solemn gloom,
't is ever sunshine, where I chant my lays.

If from my lattice low,
As evenings come and go,
The mountain tops and purple clouds I see;
Or hear the shepherd's strain,
The wind, or gentle rain,
I'm not alone – this is enough for me!

Through the hot dust of strife,
On the broad road of life,
The rhyme-paths of my youth my dim eyes fill:
When morn, and noon, and night,
Deep vale, and dizzy height,
Wore robes song-cover'd, as they ever will.

O, bliss! To turn my feet
To some old cave's retreat,
Far from the tumult of the torturing crowd;
Where nothing meets the eye,
But sea, and earth, and sky,
And Cynthia riding o'er a snow white cloud

To hear the tinkling rills,
To mark the fading hills,
To watch the light wane from the marshy moor;
To catch the labourer's song,
As home he hies along,
To kiss his children, watching by his door.

Perchance, some old weird mill,
With buckets bulged and still,
May on the common, like a Druid, stand:
Whose shadow in the lake
Shall sweet psalm-dreams awake,
Leading the muser into fairy land.

O, may this joy be mine,
Even till life's decline,
At dusk of day to watch the dwindling spire!
So, take the crowd for me;
I am content to be
Alone with Nature, and her mighty Sire!

THE BOY BARD

A thoughtful lad was miss'd one day,
And his mother had felt he was long away;
So she dropp'd her work, and closed the door,
And walk'd a little way down the moor;
And found him musing under a tree,
And cried, "Come home, my son, with me."
And the lad replied, "I will, I will;
I was learning the lore of the gentle rill.
O wist ye not that your boy hath striven
To tune the harp which the Lord hath given?"

And the words which rose on the summer air
Were treasured up by that mother there;
And those gentle tones she ever heard,
Like forest fifes by the breezes stirr'd.
Whether reading low by the evening fire,
Or spreading the meal for his labouring sire;
Whether she plied her needle bright,
Or milk'd the cow 'mid the daisies white,
In dark or light, in calm or storm,
She heard his voice, and she saw his form.

The boy grew up like a floweret wild,
For he was Nature's favourite child.
She taught him with her book of moss,
Her beetling cliff, her crag and cross,
Her sounding seas, her rivers wide,
Her hills and vales where streamlets glide,
The face of man, and blooming boy,
Or maiden, like an April joy,
Till he achieved undying fame,
And won a poet's noble name.

INTRODUCTION TO SHAKSPERE'S TERCENTENARY ODE

THE following is taken from the "Coventry Herald," April 29th, 1864:-
"The three-hundredth anniversary of the birth of Shakspere was celebrated in this city on Friday evening, April 22nd. Much interest was felt in our local festival, not only by the inhabitants of the city, but also by a large number of persons residing in various parts of the country, who had forwarded poems to compete for the two beautiful watches of Coventry manufacture which it was intended to award here on this memorable occasion. The announcement of the offering of prizes for poems was made as far back as November last, the assistance of several able men of letters having previously been obtained as adjudicators. Advertisements were inserted in a great number of literary and other journals in the metropolis, Coventry, Birmingham, and elsewhere, which resulted in a numerous list of competitors.

It was subsequently arranged that the presentation of the prizes for the poems, and the reading of the same, should form a leading feature in a commemorative entertainment to be given at the Corn Exchange on the eve of Shakspere's birthday. At five o'clock, in compliance with the Mayor's invitation, many of the shops were closed. When the entertainment commenced, the hall was about two thirds filled, many of the leading inhabitants of the town being present in evening dress. The band of the Royal Scots Greys having taken its place on the platform, a note was sounded, and Mr. Dolman came forward and pronounced in an effective manner a prologue, by Beranger, taken from Shakspere's works. The overture to 'The Merry Wives of Windsor' was then performed by the band, after which the Mayor, (R.H. Minster, Esq.,) attended by his sword and mace-bearers in their official dress, came upon the platform, and, opening the envelopes containing the names of the persons to whom the adjudicators (The Right Hon. Lord Lyttelton, G. Dawson, Esq., and C. Bray, Esq.) had awarded the prizes for the best poems on Shakspere, announced the winner of the first prize to be Mr. John Harris, of Falmouth, Cornwall. The watches were conspicuously displayed during the whole of the evening. Before the Mayor left the platform, the poem to which the first prize had been awarded was read.

Our readers may be interested to hear that the poem for which the first prize was awarded is the production of one not entirely unknown to fame. Mr. Harris is a Cornishman, whose book of poems, published some years ago, entitled 'Lays from the Mine, the Moor, and the Mountain,' received such encomiums from the leading literary journals as few poets have been favoured with.

After the reading of the poem, the Mayor left the platform, and the band played a selection from Mendelssohn's 'Midsummer Night's Dream,' which concluded the first part of the entertainment."

The "Birmingham Daily Gazette," May 12th, 1864 contains the following:-

THE SHAKSPEREAN PRIZE – The first prize was awarded to Mr. Harris on Saturday, with the following letter from Coventry:- 'May 6th, 1864. Dear Sir, – I send you by tonight's post the Gold Watch awarded to you for your poem. The watch is manufactured by one of the first English firms, Messrs. Rotherham, who have acted very liberally, and made it worth Twenty instead of Fifteen Guineas, the amount which they will be paid for it. The watch presented to the Princess of Wales was manufactured by this firm, who constantly employ upwards of two hundred hands in the different branches of the watch trade. I hope it will be satisfactory to you. J. E. M. Vincent'. – The gold watch is really a handsome one. On the centre of the case is engraven a beautiful representation of Shakspere, encircled with a wreath of leaves, and surrounded with the words, 'The Tercentenary of Shakspere, Coventry, 1864.' Inside the case are engraven those well known lines from the Great Bard:-

"Tomorrow, and tomorrow, and tomorrow
Creeps in this petty pace, from day to day,
To the last syllable of recorded time."

AN ODE

On the Anniversary of the birthday of William Shakspere,
April 23rd, 1864.
Prize Poem.

Over the earth a glow,
Peak-point and plain below,
The red round sun sinks in the purple west;
Lambs press their daisy bed,
The lark drops overhead,
And sings the labourer, hastening home to rest.

Bathed in the ruddy light,
Flooding his native height,
A youthful bard is stretch'd upon the moss;
He heedeth not the eve
Whose locks the elfins weave,
Entranced with Shakspere near a Cornish cross.

Men pass him and repass;
The hare is in the grass;
The full moon stealeth o'er the hill of pines;
Twilight is lingering dim;
The village vesper-hymn
Murmurs its music through the trembling vines.

Starts up the musing boy,
His soul is hot with joy,
He revels in a region of delight;
The winds are rich with song,
As slow they sweep along,
And earth and sky are full of holy light.

Tongues trill on every rock,
Notes flow from every block;
The hawthorn shines with fairies; the clear rill
With pointed rushes hid,
The pleasant banks amid,
Trickles its treasures tuning down the hill.

A spell is on his soul:
He scans the mystic scroll
Of human passions waken'd by the wand
Of England's noblest seer,
Whom England holds so dear, –
Great, glorious Shakspere, loved in every land!

He hears the tramp of steeds,
Sees war in gory weeds,
Roams through the forest, with delighted eyes;
Bends to the tempest's roar,
Weeps for the monarch poor,
And sobs with sorrow when dear Juliet dies.

Thus lay that musing boy,
Whose soul was hot with joy,
Environ'd in a hemisphere of rays;
And in the mystic light
The genius of the height
Brought him a lyre, which he, enraptured, plays:

He sang of him, the great,
Shakspere, of kingly state,
Who in his boyhood by clear Avon stray'd,
Learning the lore of song
From feeble thing and strong, –
The great tree towering and the tiny blade:

The welkin's solemn height,
The lightning's livid light,
The thunder's mutter, the black whirlwind's roar;
The little child at play,
The red-breast on the spray,
The daisy nodding by the ploughman's door:

The hedges, hung in flowers,
The falling, pattering showers,
The dew-drops, glittering in the morning's shine;
The smallest film that be,
Which none but poets see,
All taught him lessons with a voice Divine.

Dame Nature oped her store,
Her secret inner door;
Boldly he revell'd through her wondrous cell;
And none the song-lines read
Around and overhead,
Or knew the mystic chronicles so well.

He solved the human heart
Like mariner his chart,
And passion's every phase was known to him;
And when the full time came,
Forth burst the mighty flame,
To blaze and brighten till the stars are dim!

This greatly-gifted one
Was Labour's noblest son, –
The people's honour, leader, champion strong;
The glory of the soil,
The towering prince of toil,
The matchless monarch in the realm of song.

Loved now the wide world round,
Where human hives are found;
By prince, and peasant following the plough,
The sailor out at sea,
The yeoman on the lea,
The miner digging in the earth below:

The shepherd in his plaid,
The rosy village maid,
The warrior watching by the red camp fire;
The mother with her child,
The satchell'd schoolboy mild,
The college student, daily pressing higher:

The dweller of the street,
In the great city's heat,
The mountaineer, within his lodge of reeds;
The silent solitaire
On the wide desert bare:–
All own his witchery where the daylight speeds.

Three centuries' solemn span
Since his great life began
Have borne their burdens to the hidden sphere;
Each epoch ever found
Him with new glories crown'd,
Like the red sun when the wide west is clear.

And so, great bard, to-day
We weave thy natal lay.
And cluster gratefully around thy name:
England will ever be,
Dear Shakspere, proud of thee,
And coming ages but augment thy fame.

SONNETS TO THE MONTHS

January

The New Year wakens like a peevish child
In Winter's chamber. Nature, his dear nurse,
Rocks him upon a rolling cradle-cloud,
While the cold winds lift up their voices loud,
Filling the underworld with strainings wild, –
A tempest lullaby! In heaps up-piled
The white snow fills the land, a drapery chaste,
On mead productive, moor, and rocky waste.
Echoes the flail from the old barn of thatch,
The wild duck shelters in the frozen fen,
The redbreast hops upon the wooden latch,
And King Frost lords it o'er the icy glen.
Heap up another log. How sad to be
Abroad in such a gale on land or sea!

February

Snow-drifts and ice! Hush'd is the forest-strain,
Save the small chirrup of the busy wren.
And, like a monster moaning as in pain,
The great blast tumbles through the dreary fen,
Sweeps the bare hill, and groans along the glen.
Against the white drift on the frozen plain
The gentle snowdrop rests its drooping head;
Looking so beautiful, as if it came
From that dear land where holy angels tread.
O floweret fair, 'mid storm and whirlwind bred,
White as the cold snow which around thee lies,
How dost thou tell, when bitter winds are fled,
Of lovely wildings under genial skies,
With dew upon their lids, and sunbeams in their eyes!

March

With fresh gales rushing through the shivering trees,
Drives crashing March. The white clouds southward fly,
And up between them shine blue fields of sky.
The lark's first carol rings among the leas.
Now search the moorlands for the earliest flower,
Timidly blushing 'neath the tempest's wing,
Violet and primrose in the shelter'd bower;
While little lambs are sporting by the spring.
Beside their teams the merry plough-boys sing.
Twitter the birds where golden furze-flowers shine;
The crocus blossoms in the garden ring,
And wood and wold are full of lays Divine.
The hopeful sower sows the precious seed,
With trust in Heaven, upon the furrow'd mead.

April

With one cheek tear-wet, and the other bright
With passing sunshine, beauty in her eyes;
On her green garments buds of richest dyes;
Her fair brow bound with leaflets, in the light
Winking and shining, like a timid maid,
Blushing with freshness, seeming half afraid,
Comes changeful April. Violets fill one hand;
And these she scatters o'er the vernal land,
Studding the hedge-rows by the lone sheepfold,
And hanging gems in Nature's silent bowers.
The other doth an urn of waters hold,
Which, in soft tears, she weeps upon the flowers.
Cowslip and primrose round her neck are strung,
And Spring's first notes gush sweetly from her tongue.

May

Beautiful vestal clad in freshest green,
Fragrant with hyacinths and flowerets wild!
Of the twelve months, come, let me crown thee queen.
Lover of murmuring brooks and music mild!
The year has not a fairer, lovelier child.
Now lambs play in the fields with daisies white,
The cuckoo's voice flows full among the leaves,
The lark far up is singing out of sight,
And the glad thatcher whistles on the eaves.
The robin's nest scarce shows among the moss,
From hill and valley rings a gladsome lay,
Which floats, love-laden, over crag and cross,
And moor, and mead, and hawthorn-blossom'd way,
While Beauty walks the world. 'tis melody and May.

June

Green fields and music. Like a cheerful bard
With song surrounded, gushing where she treads,
Comes joyous June. The great trees bow their heads
Full-leaf'd. On cliffs and common hard
Are marks of Summer's fingers. Beauty-starr'd
Are all the walks of Nature: Gentle eyes
Peer out from grassy windows, and the skies
Are bridged with feathery clouds where angels glide.
Turn we to earth? The briony and rose
In the green lane are clustering side by side;
And clover-scents, in showers, are wafted wide
By village stile, and where the fountain flows.
A thousand lyres ring on the gladden'd plain,
Burst from the woods, and murmur from the main.

July

Heat and haymaking! Through the scented grass
The sharp scythe rustles, bringing music dear,
With pastoral echoes, to the listening ear;
While, in the sunshine, boy and buxom lass
Raise clover-ridges. As the gate we pass
Leading into the meadow, gales of glee
Come floating breeze-borne over lake and lea.
In the tree's shadow stand the panting kine,
Rambles the angler by the limpid stream:
The earth is full of charity Divine;
Waves the green corn where glancing swallows gleam.
The lanes are loveliness where fair things dream.
A mystery fills creation. Earth, and sea,
And fen, and forest, whisper, Lord, of Thee.

August

Ripe fruits and filberts! Over all the land
The hot air travels, bearing music bland
From shining scythe and sickle. Harvest lays
Rise where the white corn, on a hundred hills,
In the broad valleys, by the sparkling rills,
Bends to the joyous reaper; whilst a haze
Of insect incense fills the world with praise.
Wheat-waving August, in thy straw-bright hair
And leafy zone, with juicy fruitage bound,
What loveliness can with thyself compare?
Where dwells a queen so greatly, grandly crown'd?
Where'er thou tread'st, the ripe grapes cluster round.
To Him soars up one universal strain,
Who gives the early and the latter rain.

September

Behold the year's fruition! Hedges high,
And little mounds, where song-nymphs shelter shy,
Are bright with berries. Children shout for glee,
As the hedge-bramble yields them a rich store;
And ruddy apples on the orchard tree
Hang o'er the stream, or by the peasant's door.
The corn is garner'd. Down the pensive moor
The swallows glance and wheel, ere they depart
For warmer regions: skilfully they dart
O'er rock and lichen'd ruin. Here will I
Sit now and watch them. Songs of praise proceed
From grateful souls, whose hearts are beating high
By the farm-house on many a shaven mead
For harvest mercies sent in time of need.

October

Brown leaves and berries! The old woods are grand
With the decay of nature. Traces here,
Which none but poets can decipher clear;
And there are lines by the great Artist's hand.
A solemn stillness reigns o'er all the land.
Beside these elms I'll watch the skylark soar,
Which sings as though an angel met his view.
The pilgrim pauses on the pensive moor,
And strains his eyes far up the heavenly blue.
Delightful 'tis, as day is waning now,
And the last wood-bird wheels along the air
To seek his mate upon the shelter'd bough,
And spend the night in leafy safety there,
To muse on eden with its valleys fair.

November

Clouds tempest-strided, heavy-sounding rain,
Wind, darkness, cold, make up thy dismal train,
Gloomy November! How the rivers rise
And echo through the hollows! Sadly flies
The last leaf from the forest, whirling round,
Then hurl'd in anger on the sodden ground.
Sudden the change! The flowers are drown'd with tears;
The pastoral field-paths, muddy, tempt no more;
The plover on the open land appears,
And little redbreast ventures near the door;
The ploughman blows his fingers by his team,
The farmer's cart rolls rumbling down the moor.
Books now, and fire, where happy faces gleam,
And cheerful chat, when day's hard toil is o'er.

December

Like the last prophet, dark December comes,
Uttering the doom of all things. Hear, my soul,
And profit by the teacher. List the roll
Of surging waters. Not an insect hums;
Carols no bird; cold gloom fills up the whole.
The trees, leaf-stript, lift up their arms in vain
To catch the struggling sunshine. On their steeds
The winds are mounted, prancing o'er the plain,
Then up the hills, then down the vales again.
Like a tried friend returning through the meads
He lov'd in childhood, after absence long,
To cheer us with his converse, even so
Comes blessed Christmas with its holy song
To gladden once again this world of woe.

The Seasons

With virgin Spring he travelled arm in arm,
Watching her trickery with buds and flowers,
A conquered captive by her magic charm,
Her gentle breezes and her vernal showers,
When larks sang sweetly over violet bowers,
And linnets twittered on the sprouting tree;
To Monro these were more delightful hours
Than any others in the year could be,
And in a fresher strain his simple songs sang he.

He loved the Summer for her robe of green,
Her wayside gems, and leafy forests grand,
Her wealth of roses in the noon's full sheen,
When bursts of gladness travel o'er the land;
And Autumn, with the dry leaves in his hand
O'erwritten with the stanzas of the wood,
When the rich grapes, by amorous zephyrs fanned,
Hang by the porch, and cluster near the flood,
Speaking in wisdom's ear that God to all is good.

And Old Man Winter had his charms as well,
The fairy frost-work glittering on the pane,
The snow-flakes falling in the hollow dell,
Or ranked in drifts upon the open plain,
The plover's cry, the robin's liquid strain,
When sunlight gleamed, beside his cottage door,
The cowboy's whistle in the sheltered lane,
Or the warm log-light falling on the floor,
All these illumed his thought and added to his store.

The time of early budding was his choice,
When Nature roused herself from winter's sleep,
And through the woodlands rang a gladsome voice,
And golden sunbeams glittered on the steep.
The opening blossoms caused his heart to leap,
And the first primrose by the watching meres,
Like a fond mother long time led to weep
For a lost child throughout the lagging years,
Returning swiftly home to wipe away her tears.

Mining Toil

Then came the darkness of the dangerous mine,
His daily, nightly tasks of tedious toil,
Where never star, or moon, or sunbeams shine,
But sulphur-wreaths around the caverns coil,
Which health, and strength, and mental might dispoil,
Giving the feet of time a tardy pace,
Through heated hollows and rude rifts to moil,
When boyhood's blossoms opened on his face,
And greenness clothed the tree which gave his being grace.

And what he saw, and what he suffered there,
By day and night, can never be expressed,
Where sulphur-furies thronged the sickly air,
And Danger burrowed in the blackest vest,
Mid rocks which rent to aid his mineral-quest,
Exploding holes, and shafts as dark as doom,
Where hollow echoes sink into the breast,
And solemn breathings hurry through the gloom,
Like those which wizards say are murmuring from the tomb.

Sometimes his arms were heavy with his task,
So that 'twas hard to lift them to his head,
His face like one who wore a dismal mask,
Of black, or white, or yellow, brown, or red.
Exhausted oft, he made the flints his bed,
And dreamt of groves of olives far away,
By dews divine and gales of gladness fed,
Where sunlight glitters all the livelong day,
And harpers mid the trees and falling waters play.

The heat, the cold, the sulphur and the slime,
The grinding masses of the loosened rock,
The scaling ladders, the incessant grime
From the dank timbers and the dripping block,
The lassitude, the mallet's frequent knock,
The pain of thirst when water was so near,
The aching joints, the blasted hole's rude shock,
Could not dash out the music from his ear,
Or stay the sound of song which ever murmured clear.

The cavern's sides, the vagues of shining spar,
The roof of rock where scarce the candle gleams,
The hollow levels strangely stretching far
Beneath the mountains, full of mineral seams,
Were evermore to him befitting themes,
For meditation and his rustic lay;
While in the darkness his pale visage gleams,
To read rich sonnets on the furrowed clay,
And craggy slabs that jut the ladder's lonely way.

Thus month by month, and tedious year by year,
This heavy mining darkness closed him round,
So far away from all he held most dear,
The rocky hillside and the lower ground,
Where the dear wild flowers blushed so sweetly round,
And taught him more than books, or learned men,
And all their creeds and axioms profound,
Although propounded by the page or pen;
A higher voice he heard in every glade and glen.

My Native Hearth

My native hearth, my native hearth!
Blest be the spot which gave me birth!
Blest be the roof that shelter'd me
In the sweet hours of infancy!
Blest be the rock, the heath, the glen!
Blest be the eye that watch'd me then;
My mother's eye, that on me stream'd,
When in the cradle soft I dream'd;
The kiss vouchsafed in accent meek,
Leaving its love-trace on my cheek!
Blessed, thrice blessed, be the hand
That led me o'er my fatherland!
His voice, though silent in the tomb,
Is heard amid my mountain broom.
He watch'd me when my infant eye
Was roaming through the starry sky;
And told me, as our Mount we trod,
"The moon and stars were made by God."
His words impress'd my opening youth
With thoughts of Deity and truth,
Were graven on my early life,
Are with me now in manhood's strife;
They murmur in my musing dream,
By open heath or sobbing stream;
I hear them from the churchyard's sod,
"The moon and stars were made by God."

My native hearth, my native hearth!
Blest be the home where I had birth,
My mountain home, of homes the best,
Upon the old hill's heathy crest!
Time-eaten cot, thy rented wall
Will surely very shortly fall;
Thy ragged roof and casements grey
Will surely soon be swept away.
The rushing blast, with dismal groan,
Will o'er thy prostrate ruins moan;
And where was heard the poet's song,
The angry winds will scowl along.
Blest be the hearth-stone where the flower
First blossom'd in its heather-bower;
And where the wind-rock'd mountain shoots
First nodded on their striking roots;
Where oft, beside the taper pale,
My mother told her pleasing tale
At winter-time, when girl and boy
Look'd up and smiled, brimful of joy!
Blest be ye all ! I weep to see
Your ruin-rented destiny.
If through the red man's woods I roam,
I'll weep for thee, my mountain home;
Fly from the din of noise and mirth,
To muse upon my native hearth.

Cornwallia

Twilight with me, twilight with thee:
No morn my strength restores,
As when, companioned with my harp,
I wandered down thy moors,
And heard, where bowers were ivy-roofed,
Cross-streaked with sunset hues,
When boyhood roved among thy meads,
The mysteries of the Muse.

From morn till eve, from youth to age,
Till green leaves turned to brown,
Have I, enamoured of thy charms,
Gone crooning up and down,
Until thy streams and bye-ways still
And solemn commons wide
Were like the faces of my flock
Around my own fireside.

When moonlight-shafts fell on thy meres,
And fairies thronged thy wells,
How oft I've heard the queen of song
Within thy flowery dells!
And where thy mineral stores lie hid
Beneath the pall of night,
Mine ears have caught unuttered strains
From many a tinselled sprite.

In glens where giants lived in caves,
And princes stalked of yore,
I've stayed my feet to hear the rush
Of armies on the shore,
Where now the glancing swallows wheel
Till glows the red sunset
Along thy craggy castled peaks,
Or fisher plies his net.

How many cells from man retired,
Where no one sees or hears,
How many moss-banks, fay-impressed,
I've hallowed with my tears,

When Eve led Silence down the hills
Into the dingles dim,
And God was pleading on the heights
That men should turn to Him!

Twilight with me, twilight with thee:
Yet still thy waters roar,
And great ships come and great ships go
With many a precious store.
Thy mountain-tarns are sacred sites,
Thy peaks are holy ground,
Where angels gather in the dusk
When psalms are floating round.

From schoolboy tasks to fading age,
Thy reeds and rocks among,
Muse-led, my earnest life has been
An era of strange song.
My theme – thy beauties unsurpassed
On sea-side, mead, and moor,
Where fairest damsels sing thy fame
By many a rustic door.

Yet though I hear the sound of strings
Among thy rustling reed,
And voices whispering in thy pines,
Men give but little heed.
And if I tell them song is there,
So many turn their head,
And almost offer me a stone
In lieu of daily bread.

Twilight with me, twilight with thee:
Yet will I sing thy worth
Until thou yieldest me a grave
Within my mother earth.
The flowers are fair in other lands,
And clear the waters fall,
But old Cornwallia is the best
And brightest of them all.

To My Bower

Dear natural bower! What a pleasure to greet
Thy heath-hanging roof and thy moss-cover'd seat!
'tis not very long I have fled from thy sight;
Yet since, in perspective, I've seen thee so bright,
So clothed with thy mantle of sky-coloured light,
That I'd leave the great world at this tear-dropping hour,
Could I muse once again in my heath-cover'd bower!

From the chit-chat of life how delicious to steal
To this grotto of quiet, my sadness to heal!
'tis like balm to my spirit, like rest to my frame,
When I gaze on the heath whence my forefathers came.
How familiar each rock in its ivy-clad throne!
How each hedge to my eye-ball distinctly is known!
How I love the fresh breeze! How I prize the young flower
That smiles forth at spring in my heath-cover'd bower!

How sweet in this cave of retirement to kneel,
When the hallowing awe of devotion I feel,
And when to the God of my being I pray,
Who has guided me over life's thorn-piercing way!
How delicious the feast 'neath the mantle of even,
To drink of the streamlet meandering from heaven!
'tis a sacred retreat where the song-spirits cower;
They sing their soft lays in my heath-cover'd bower!

We've been friends a long time in sorrow and glee;
Each day thou art dearer and dearer to me.
I love thee so well, I cannot but sigh
When I think, – O, how sad! – we must part by and bye.
The sigh of the rill in the distance is heard,
And mingled with this is the plaint of the bird;
A seraph's bright pinions are brooding above,
And around me is floating the music of love;
Angelical lays, on the drops of the shower,
Fall down from the sky in my heath-cover'd bower!

And when the wan moon, from her throne in the sky,
Gilds the mountain's crisp heath-locks that rustle hard by;
When the sky-lark has hung his mute lyre on the cloud,
And the light dews are dropping on twilight's dim shroud;
When under the hawthorn my closet is made,
And I look to my Father, imploring his aid;
Methinks I then feel such a life-giving power,
As lifts me to heaven from my heath-cover'd bower!

Man bows down to something he dares to enshrine,
Around which forever his heart-strings entwine, –
Some being angelic, some angel of worth,
Some sacred retreat, some green nook of this earth:
Ay, he clings, ever clings, to the place of his birth!
The home of his childhood, though oceans may sever,
Possesseth those charms which attract him for ever.
And I have one spot, Nature's bountiful dower,
The sweetest of all:– 't is my heath-cover'd bower!

What a peaceable spot! Not a motion of strife
Disturbs you, or ripples the current of life.
The din of the city affrights you no more:
At peace you may talk with the heroes of yore,
With spirits that long have departed on high,
To the home of the blest in the star-dotted sky!
'tis the fane of the Muse, where no sadness can lower:
The breezes have lyres in my heath-cover'd bower!

It may not attract you, when seen from afar;
But to me it shines forth like a beautiful star.
'tis more precious to me, the lone warbling one,
Than the wood-waving land where my kindred have gone.
I would dwell in this heath-nook my life's little day;
And when the tired spirit shall flutter away,
O lay me to rest where will bloom the wild flower,
And the breezes sing sweet, – in my heath-cover'd bower!

To a Cluster of Primroses

Your graces have been sung
Bards of sweetest strain;
But this shall tune my humble lyre, –
I see you once again!
I see you peeping forth
Beneath the budding trees,
And I adore the Mighty One
Who made such flowers as these!

Stars of the wakening dell,
Ye constellations bright,
How like the eyes of those we love
Ye steal upon the sight!
Blushing in solitude,
Where Peace and Silence reign,
Ye early children of the spring,
I see you once again!

Ye come and pass away,
As gayer roses do!
For many friends, since last spring-tide,
Have pass'd away with you.
In this sweet primrose-dell,
Ye blossom but to wane:
Thank God for His preserving care, –
I see you once again!

A little while ago,
These banks were very dry;
But now they are the loveliest spots
Beneath the April sky.
And since I see you here,
O let me not complain,
But put my trust in Providence; –
I see you once again!

Chaste, lovely little things!
Dame Nature nurses you;
Ye quaff the breeze that murmurs by,
And drink the falling dew:
And 'tis my faith that He
Who made the Primrose-flower,
Can raise my body from the dust
To bloom in Eden's bower!

The Child's First Prayer

Weary with play, the little boy
Unto his mother ran,
Who kiss'd his pretty smiling face
As only mother can:
And, bending o'er her little one,
She wept, although she smiled,
And taught him this, his first sweet prayer, –
"Our Father, bless thy child!"

Among the dewy flowers of May
He and his mother walk'd:
Summers and winters had pass'd by: –
How lovingly they talk'd!
Sweet was the music of their lips
That so the hour beguiled:
He knelt among the flowers, and said,
"Our Father, bless thy child!"

Behold him in the churchyard shed
Tears, bitter tears of woe:
His mother weeps beside him, too: –
His father is laid low!
But suddenly he stills the storm
Of bursting passion wild;
And, bending o'er the grave, he says,
"Our Father, bless thy child!"

He stood upon a foreign shore,
To stately manhood grown;
His mother to the better land
A long, long time had flown.
And here, where Nature's sentinels
In frowning ranks were filed,
He raised his eyes to heaven, and said,
"Our Father, bless thy child!"

This, through the changing scene of life,
Did not from memory part;
His mother's voice was in his ear,
Her lesson in his heart.
And wheresoe'er his lot might be,
In storms and tempests wild,
This was the pilgrim's sweetest prayer, –
"Our Father, bless thy child!"

His locks were silver'd o'er with age,
And dim his watery eye,
When, on a Christian Sabbath-eve,
He laid him down to die.
He fell asleep so peacefully,
And, O! so sweetly smiled,
And whisper'd with his dying breath,
"Our Father, bless thy child!"

The First Violet

Hail to thee, little flower,
Within my mountain bower,
Smiling among the wiry broom,
Like Hope's bright star 'mid
clouds of gloom!
I bend me o'er thy sweet blue eye,
Dropping salt tears I know not why,
Feeling a warm inspiring fire,
Sweeping my fingers o'er my lyre,
Singing within my heathy bower:
Hail, hail to thee, Spring's early flower!

Yes, thou art come to dwell
With Memory in her cell,
To call her from her still retreat,
And place Remembrance at her feet.
Though thou art gilt with vernal bloom,
Thou tellest of the dark, deep tomb:
Thou tellest of the wide blue sea,
Where waves and storms are wont to be,
And where upon its boundless tide,
Far, far away my kindred ride.
Because they hasten from my bower,
Hail, hail to thee, Spring's early flower!

O, could they hear the lark,
Singing till it is dark,
Fluttering his wings those meads above,
And warbling forth his notes of love;
And could they, in our garden's bound,
Gaze on these cowslips scatter'd round,
See all those daisies on the plain;
They surely would come back again,
To feast their eyes within my bower
Upon my little violet-flower!

What were the words I said?
Thou speakest of the dead?
Ah, yes! Thou tellest of decay,
How earthly splendours pass away:
An hour or two, – come, smile on me, –
And I shall bid farewell to thee.
Here birds will sing, and
flowers will bloom,
When I am hidden in the tomb.
But I would sleep with thee, sweet flower,
Companions in my heather-bower.

And oft my ghost shall roam
Around my mountain-home;
And here, beneath the wan moon's light,
Weave heath-crowns for the brow of Night.
Blue herald of a numerous line!
Thou'rt stamp'd with the great
Maker's sign,
The impress of the Hand Divine:
Bending thou seem'st to kiss the sod:
Who sees thee, sees a ray of God.
Because He shines within my bower,
Hail, hail to thee, Spring's early flower!

To the Swallow

Welcome, welcome, little swallow,
Floating round my heathy hollow,
Stooping down to kiss the flower
Bordering my heather-bower!
Many a by-gone tale thou bringest,
As away, away thou wingest,
Gliding o'er my native heath,
Sweeping down the vale beneath;
Through the merry meads thou strayest,
With my mountain's locks thou playest;
Now above my head thou wheelest,
Not through yonder dell thou stealest.
Welcome, welcome, little swallow,
Floating round my heathy hollow!

Bird of bright and glossy wing,
Coming to us in the spring!
Dost thou love this nook so rude?
'tis the cave of solitude.
Here I've linger'd many an hour;
Bird, this is the poet's bower!
Float around me, little stranger;
Float around me, – there's no danger.
Startling sounds won't here alarm thee:
Can a poet's musings harm thee?
Other birds, the woods among,
Cheer us with their summer-song;
But thou'rt welcome, little swallow,
Floating round my heathy hollow!

THE SONNETS

MORNING

How beautiful, beneath yon eastern cloud,
Hung like a porter by the gates of Day,
The breezy Morning opes its eye of grey,
Lifting from off the earth Night's murky shroud!
How freshly from the mountains comes the breeze;
Fanning the robe of Summer, gemm'd with flowers;
Shaking the dew-drops from the forest-trees,
And whispering sweetly in the wakening bowers!
The robin stirs among the trembling leaves,
And up the mountain scuds the timid hare;
The sparrows chatter on the shaven eaves,
O'er which the graceful smoke-wreaths curl so fair;
The rising sky-lark sings to greet the dawn,
And the blithe mower whistles on the lawn.

EVENING

Hail, quiet Evening! 'Neath thy gathering vest
Musing I rove. How sweet, within my ken,
The rural hamlet down the peaceful glen,
Yon white-wash'd cottage smiling in the west,
The fragrant meadows, budding trees all dress'd
In early beauty; while the throstle's note
Doth on the downy wings of Twilight float!
Now the sweet flowers their dewy lids are closing,
The "glimmering landscape" from my sight recedes.
See Contemplation by the rill reposing,
And mark dull Silence hovering round the meads:
Peace leads the breezes o'er the shadowy dale,
And Fancy flits with fairies through the reeds,
Whilst distant hymnings murmur in the vale.

NIGHT

How awful are thy "trailing" robes, O Night!
How solemn is thy breathing! how profound
The mystic voice that seems to travel round,
Like holiest hymnings from some distant sprite!
The labourers of yon hamlet are asleep:
I, 'neath the pale moon, wander on and weep.
Now all is silent, save the night-bird's song,
Or the sweet music of the tinkling rill;
And while I, wondering, gaze the stars among,
And toil delighted up this gorse-clad hill,
My thoughts are roaming wide mid sacred things;
The past comes back upon me:– friends are here,
Departed ones, for whom I've shed the tear:–
Methinks I catch the rustling of their wings.

CAMBORNE

Time chisels out the foot-prints of the Past,
Planing away old hieroglyphic scars,
Gashing strange notches in his calendar,
And raising, on the ashes of an hour,
New wonders, to be wondrous and decay.

How like a thing of magic hast thou rose
Out of the copper-caverns of the earth,
Graceful and plain, poetically neat, –
The cottage-homes of those that work below,
Where Sun, or star, or silver-margin'd cloud,
Or tree, or flower, or bird, or murmuring brook,
Or chiming breeze, or tuneful waterfall,
Is never seen or heard! How like a thing
That leap'd into existence at a nod,
Art thou, my native Camborne! girded round
With mead, and meadow-land, and shady grove,
And boundary-lines of sweetest earthly bliss!

I well remember, in my childish days
Thy name was like a magic word to me,
Replete with strange emotion! Not a lip
That syllabled the word but seem'd to be
More than a common hero; And I thought,
If I could stand upon thy threshold-stones,
And peep into thy streets of burnish'd brass,
"Glittering and flashing" in the golden sun,
Why, I should see just all the world at once; –
O Camborne! What a blessed sight for me!

I came, – was led along thy narrow streets,
Stood in thy porches, heard the hum of those
Who long have slept beneath the grassy sod,
Gazed at thy toy-shop windows, – gazed and gazed,
Until I thought the little horses moved,
And snapped their bitless bridles! then again
Rubb'd both mine eyes to see the gingerbread,

Like gilded soldiers marching on the stall,
With lions, tigers, bears, and elephants,
And images of beasts before the Flood,
Grotesque and strange, wild, knotty, limbless things;
So that I leap'd and clapp'd my hands for joy;
And, when I sat again on mother's knee,
I thought that I had realised my dream,
Had seen the very centre of the world,
And knew all bright and precious things were there,
And told her stories three or four months long.

Old time, since then, has dragg'd me by the hand
O'er mountain-heights, through briers and tangled thorns,
And over slippery crags, where Danger scream'd,
And flapp'd his ebon wings, and scream'd again;
Has torn the scales from off mine opening lids
With his long bony fingers, one by one,
Till, in reflection's sober light, I see
My childhood's wonder wonderful no more!
And now I walk along thy crowded streets,
And mingle sometimes in thy busy mart,
With my loved harp upon my shoulder slung,
Unknown, unnoticed! Not a peasant-boy,
Wheeling his cabbages across the street,
Believes me, clad in labour's homely weeds,
And following in his train, a singing one,
Who loves the music of all whispering things.

Thou hast thy halls of learning, and thy men
Of wonderful renown; thou ownest too
Thy seats of science, and thy mounts of power,
Thy dens of discord, and thy bowers of bliss,
Thy hallow'd fanes, and dungeons dark and deep.
Thou hast, within thy borders, master-minds,
Rare spirits, of the modern mining school,
Who, mole-like, dig their way into the earth,
Yoking the elements in brotherhood,
To belch the flashing diamond into light,
And vomit forth the backbone of the world!

Thou hast thy men of letters. One there is,*
A monarch in the kingdom of the mind,
Who knew thee in thy young, infantile days,
And frolick'd with thy lovely Cornish vest,
Weaving thy tresses in his summer-dreams.
Ay, one there is whose name will never die,
Till the last trump shall rattle on the blast,
And Time himself grow feverish, and expire.
See'st thou his dwelling, on the green hill's side,
Like a calm king-bird, ever looking down
Upon thy temple-tops? Ay, he shall live,
And only fall with Nature's funeral fire!

Thou hast thy solemn grave-yard, and thy tombs,
Where lie the ashes of our pilgrim-sires,
Grass-cover'd graves, and some without a blade,
Trees weeping dew-drops at the vesper time,
And flowers that tell us all is calm below.
Here rich and poor are "huddled out of sight,"
And sweetly sleep together; not a sigh
Disturbs the halcyon of their dreamless rest!
Without its pale, a thousand voices roar
And hiss unmeaning torture! but, within,
A solemn silence sits on every bough,
And creeps with silken feet along the grass;
Voices, unseen, are whispering to the soul;
And in the tower are heard the feet of Death.

It is for this I love thee; for I've thought,
Ay, often thought, that my last sleep should be
In the still churchyard of my native town!
Here lie my sire and grandsire, side by side;
And here a little sister, a span long;
And I have thought, – but no, it must not be;
O let me moulder where my daughter sleeps! –
That I would hang my wild harp o'er my tomb,
And go to sleep beside them! Fare thee well!
The silver moon unveils her lovely face,
And gazes down upon thy twilight bowers,

* *George Smith, F.A.S.*

As if she really loved thee! flinging floods
Of silver pencillings across thy robes,
And bathing thee in beauty! O, 'tis sweet
Here in the moonlight to look down and see
The moonbeams dancing on thy cottage-roofs!
It will be even so when we are gone,
And sleeping in our graves. – Once more, farewell!

The Haymakers Song

"Toss, toss the hay!
't is beautiful, in the summer-time,
When sweet July is in its prime,
To carol in the meads my rhyme,
And toss the hay.

"Toss, toss the hay!
The lark has sung his matin-song,
The sun is shining bright and strong,
And swallows sport the trees among:
"Toss, toss the hay!

"Toss, toss the hay!
The bard has stretch'd him in the shade,
And yonder walks the village maid,
In flowers of golden broom array'd:
"Toss, toss the hay!

"Toss, toss the hay!
Who will, may dig the shining ore;
Who will, may toil on foreign shore;
Who will, may dye their blades in gore:
We'll toss the hay!

"Toss, toss the hay!
And when our pleasant task is done,
And down has sunk the setting sun,
Among the low stacks we will run:
"Toss, toss the hay!

"Toss, toss the hay!
Long life to all who guide the plough,
Who wield the scythe, and rear the mow,
Or fling the grass, as we do now:
"Toss, toss the hay!"

TRESLOTHAN

How alter'd are thy features, Quietude,
Since erst upon thy lap at eventide,
Or in the cot of Hospitality,
Or by the margin of thy infant rill,
I swept the poets lyre! A change has come:
Thy mead a burial-ground, where friend and foe
Lie slumbering 'neath thine ivy-shining walls.
How alter'd are thy features, Quietude!
Change has been revelling with thy rustic robes, –
Not as she does in ruin-rented halls,
Shaking the turrets with her gusty blast,
And gnawing down the iron battlement
As easily as one can crop a flower:
Not as she does upon my mountain's head,
Tearing the heath-locks from its wrinkled pate,
To decorate the spirit of the blast,
Raving and roaring round my crumbling cot.
No; not like this, but clothing thee in smiles,
With pencillings as fair as Art can give,
And tricking thee as for thy bridal-hour.

I well remember in my early days
How beautiful thou wert! A cot or two
Just peeping through thy shining robe of leaves,
And shedding on the' enchanted traveller
Sweet showers of nectar from the garden-rose.
Ay, one there was, more beautiful than all,
Which lingers with me as a glittering gem
Amid the shadowy vistas of the past,
The happy home of poetry and love!
Alas! How changed! The voice of song has ceased,
And hearts unstirr'd by music slumber there.
The silent wallflower, as I hie along,
Looks sadly on me with its weeping eyes,
Unpruned, untended, fluttering in the breeze,
And sighing for the hand that nurtured it.

That hand is frozen with the frost of death,
In the damp grave beneath an aged tree.
Oft in the twilight have I wander'd here,
Far from the turmoil of the noisy crowd,
And, resting on thy grave-stones, harp in hand,
Have wept and wept again, and wish'd at last
My bones should rest in this sequester'd spot
With those I love on earth. So let it be.

Peace to thy shade, Eliza! Slumber on,
Where noise and riot never dare intrude.
The sigh that rends the heart-strings, and the sob
Riving the walls of the clay tenement,
And shaking furiously life's prison-house,
Will never rack thy peaceful bosom more.
Peace to thee, gentle sleeper! May the friends
That planted o'er thy head the early rose, –
So emblematic of the Muses' child, –
And he who drops at eventide the tear,
Rejoin thee in the skies! O, when I think
Thy spirit is in heaven clad in white robes,
And o'er the flowery banks of Paradise
Gliding with angel-bands, hymning His praise
Who bought thee with His blood, methinks I feel
Increased desires to do my Maker's will,
That, when I die, we both may meet again
In sweet companionship, – to part no more.

To the Old Hill

Once more to climb thy rocky brow,
  When early buds are peeping;
Once more to muse where breezes blow,
  And white young lambs are leaping;
To brush thy hair through croft and mead,
  Refresh'd with vernal rain;
  O, this is luxury indeed,
  And glads my heart again!

Once more, and yet once more, old hill,
  I kneel upon thy crest:
Of all those mountain-peaks around,
  Thou art the brightest, best.
The flowers that gem thy rustling locks,
  And stud thy forehead fair,
Are peering from among the rocks,
  To me beyond compare.

Once more, my native mount, once more
  The welcome Spring is come:
How freshly steal the soft south winds
  Along my mountain home!
And flowers, as when a boy, come forth,
  Clinging to moss and stone;
But ah! they look a different look,
  And speak a different tone.

Once more, within my quiet bower,
  I hear the sky-lark's song:
How wildly come his warblings down,
  Those heather-brakes among!
Bless'd be the God of Providence!
  His name will I adore,
Who spares me on my pilgrim-way
  To visit thee once more.

To My Children

Joyous, sportive, careless things,
  Floating by, like silver wings,
Gliding round my humble shed,
Blessings, blessings on your head!
O what golden cords ye twine
Round this bleeding heart of mine!
  O! the music of your voice
  Bids the mourning one rejoice,
And your sunny glances throw
Glorious summer round my brow.
Blessings on ye! Glide around,
Making home enchanted ground;
  Prattle, carol by mine hearth,
Beauteous gems of richest worth!
  I will hang upon my lyre,
  With my fingers on the wire,
Smiling, through the falling tear,
  That ye are so happy here.

What would home, and all its cares,
  Be without your simple airs?
  Be without your loving kiss,
Sweeteners of domestic bliss?
Ye are all my earthly wealth, –
Stars in darkness, suns in health, –
Flowers whose healing odours rise
  Like the gales of Paradise.
  If it were my fate to dwell
In some humble cloister'd cell,
Poor and needy, friendless too,
I would still rejoice with you.
  Blessings on ye! May you be
  Friends of want and misery!
May you live, sweet ones, to throw
Nectar on the wounds of woe,
Live the Christian's boon to find,
  Live to benefit mankind!

On the Death of My Daughter Lucretia
(who died December 23rd 1855, aged six years and five months.)

And art thou gone so soon?
And is thy loving, gentle spirit fled?
Ah! Is my fair, my passing beautiful,
My loved Lucretia number'd with the dead?
Ah! Art thou gone so soon?

I miss thee, daughter now,
In the dear nooks of earth we oft have trod;
And a strange longing fills my yearning soul
To sleep with thee, and be, like thee, with God!
I miss thee, daughter, now.

I miss thee at thy books,
Lisping sweet Bible-accents in my ear,
Showing me pictures by the evening lamp,
Beautiful emblems thou didst love so dear:
I miss thee at thy books.

I miss thee at thy prayers,
When the eve-star is looking through the sky,
And thy lone sister kneels in sorrow down,
To pray to her great Father up on high:
I miss thee at thy prayers.

I miss thee by the brook,
Where we have wander'd many a summer's day,
And thou wert happy with thy loving sire,
More happy here than at thy simple play:
I miss thee by the brook.

I miss thee in the Reenes*
Where we have hasted in the twilight dim
To wake the echoes of the silent dell,
And mark the glow-worm 'neath the hawthorn's limb:
I miss thee in the Reenes.

Reenes – A beautiful local dell

I miss thee on the hill,
The dear old hill which we have climb'd so oft;
And O, how very happy have we been
In the still bower of the old heathy croft!
I miss thee on the hill.

I miss thee at day's close,
When from my labour I regain my cot,
And sit down sadly at the supper-board,
Looking for thee, but, ah! I see thee not:
I miss thee at day's close.

I miss thee every where, –
In my small garden, watching the first flower, –
By the clear fountain, – in thy Sunday-class, –
Running to meet me at the evening-hour:
I miss thee every where.

Farewell, my beautiful!
Thy sinless spirit is with Christ above:
Thou hast escaped the evils of the world:
We have a daughter in the meads of love.
Farewell, my beautiful!

When I and little Jane
Walk hand in hand along the old hill's way,
Shall we not feel thy cherub-presence, love,
Singing our sad psalms in the twilight grey?
I soon shall go to thee.

Companion of the bard,
Mid rocks and trees, and hedges ivy-cross'd!
At morn and eve in Nature's presence-cell
We oft have enter'd with our musings lost,
My child, my harp, and I.

How thou didst love the flowers,
The mountain-heather and the buds of Spring,
The brooks and birds, the hush of solitude,
The moon and stars, like some diviner thing,
Beautiful prophetess!

Ah! Thou wert like a rose,
Dropp'd by an angel on earth's feverish clime,
To bloom full lovely, till December winds
Blasted thy beauty in its morning's prime,
Ere it had half unclosed!

Hush, murmuring spirit, hush!
It is the Lord, He only, who hath given;
And He hath taken – blessed be His name! –
The gem, which fell from paradise, to heaven:
I bow and kiss His rod.

To the Hawthorn

Flower-cover'd hawthorn! In thy tuneful shade,
My day's work done, I lay myself along.
The shepherd loves thee; hind and village maid
Full often carol here their evening song.
As float the vesper-notes those dells among,
And the red light is streaming through the glades,
I gaze and weep, – weep with excess of joy!
Nature is mine; her features never cloy.
Song-honour'd hawthorn, fairy of the mead,
Gem of the mountain, beauty of the vale!
Here the young lover tells his tender tale;
And here the poet pipes his artless lay,
Under thy branches whistling on his reed,
Forgetting all who "fill life's dusty way."

HUMOROUS PIECES

To My Old Silk Hat

Poor weather-beaten silker, how slight thou'rt looking now,
From what thou wert seven years ago, when perch'd upon my brow!
Thy shagless top, and silkless brim, how piteous to behold!
And sides, that look crush'd cruelly together with the cold!

Thou didst not always look like this, poor, ragged, wrinkled wight!
When thou wert brought from Paris here, thou wast a beauty quite;
Thy glossy silken self might then grace even a *captain's* brow;
But Time hath torn thee in his rage: thou'rt sadly alter'd now.

For seven long years, old holeless friend, we've travell'd up and down,
And thou hast been content to wane on my rhyme-ridden crown.
The angry storms have fought with thee among the granite rocks:
And none but silkers such as thou could stand the winter-shocks.

Change after change has alter'd both my old silk hat and me,
Since first we met, ay, proudly met, elate in youthful glee;
But signs have been for months gone by that thou wouldst surely fall,
While hanging to thy wonted nail, escutcheon'd in my hall.

I know not who thy maker was, nor what his name might be:
For once he did outdo himself, when he had fashion'd thee.
A Paris hat to stand the rust and rub of such an age
Adds glory to the Frenchman's name, unknown in history's page!

To a Mouse
which had eaten the leaves of my Lexicon.

How darest thou, soft-footed elf,
With tiny open jaw,
To cram such crooked syllables
Into thy greedy maw?
Would not some common
household-words
Such joy to thee afford,
Or crumbs that fall at supper-time
From off our humble board?

The woodman yonder with his axe
Look on this book with dread,
Pronounces it an oracle,
And shakes his hoary head.
He would not mar this mystic page,
't would cripple his belief;
But thou, fur-cover'd sinner, com'st
And eat'st it leaf by leaf.

What strange mice-spells thy
deeds will wake,
When in your mossy nook,
Surrounded with thy mute compeers,
Thou talkest of my book!
Will not thy grandsire shake his head,
To hear what thou hast done?
Disturb a poet in his dreams!
O thou degenerate son!

Take care, word eating pilferer,
What learned meals thou 'rt at!
If I can catch thee nibbling books,
I'll give thee to the cat.
Some two-legg'd mice, like thee,
sleek rogue!
Climb where they have no right,
Eat what belongs to other men,
And vanish out of sight.

MINOR POEMS

Lost and Found

The garden-gate wide open swung;
A blooming pair passed by;
The old man 'neath the beech-tree sat
With sorrow in his eye.
He heeded not the lark o'erhead;
His gaze was on the ground:
For he that morn his daughter lost,
And she a husband found.

He watched them down the lonely lane,
And o'er the village stile,
Beyond the hollow by the wood
Where honeysuckles smile;
And birds were singing by the brook,
And whistling on the trees;
And oft the maiden's handkerchief
Was waving on the breeze.

Full soon beyond the old man's view
The youthful couple pass'd:
He dropped his face upon his hands,
And tears fell free and fast;
And other days came back to him
With hopes and fears sublime
When earth with buds was beautiful,
And love was in its prime.

And then a mystic stillness fell
Upon his waiting soul,
And echoes from the higher hills
Over his spirit stole.
He lifted up his furrowed face, –
Serene it was and mild, –
And breathed these earnest words of prayer:
"O Heaven, direct my child!"

Days passed, and months, and then there came
A little stranger fair,
With million mysteries in her eyes,
Soft cheek and shining hair;
And smallest feet were toddling round
Upon his cottage floor,
And sunny smiles went up to him,
And he was glad once more.

And thus the tale of human life
For evermore is told:
To-day the sky is overcast,
To-morrow tinged with gold.
One joy departs, another comes
To fill the vacant place;
And so 'twill be till death assails
The last of Adam's race.

Come-to-Good (Inscribed to Lovell Squire)

I knew not, though I've lingered long
Through dear Cornubia's glades of song,
By tinkling stream fair-fringed with moss,
By crag and carn and curious cross,
That our own land of wild and wood
Owned sweet sequestered Come-To-Good.

Yet here it is, with lawn outspread,
With brook and breeze and dew-cup fed,
Where twittering birds from bush and brake
Their ever-murmuring notes awake
O'er many a pilgrim's grassy mound
Within the humble burial-ground.

And sleep they low on beds of clay,
When roses bloom, when leaves decay,
Watched by the ever-spreading sky,
The silver moon, the stars on high,
Till on the resurrection morn
They rise, on angel-wings upborne.

The hue of Spring is on the earth,
Which feels again a living birth,
Green shoots and flowers from hill to hill,
From creek to creek, from rill to rill;
While wandering cuckoo's welcome note
Doth o'er the golden furze-flowers float.

Here stands in reed-roof fair to see
That meeting-house beside the lea,
With shaven eaves and lattice low,
Where George Fox preached so long ago,
And where from lips by Heaven unsealed
We heard the Saviour's love revealed.

O Come-To-Good! O temple meet
To bow in silence at His feet!
O fitting place for bard to dwell,
And wake the mysteries of his shell;
Where bank and bower, and lawn and lea,
And wood and water, tell of Thee!

The Heroic Miner

The world has real heroes,
Whose minds with truth are stored,
Who never bled in battle,
Who never wielded sword:
True helpers of the people,
In moral warfare strong;
Whose lives have passed unheeded,
Whose names are not in song.

And such I deem the miner
Who, when his work was done,
Ascended in the bucket,
He and his little son.
O, how they fondly chatted,
As up the shaft they sped,
Of those who waited for them
Where their own board was spread!

When, hark! a crack which fills them
With sharp and sudden pain:
The rope, the rope is breaking, –
Two strands are snapped in twain;
One, only one remaineth, –
The strain doth it destroy;
It cannot bear much longer
That father and his boy.

O noble, noble parent!
"Sit still, my child," said he.
"'t will bear you up in safety,
And do not grieve for me."
And then that loving father
Sprang out into the gloom,
And found within the darkness
A Christian hero's tomb.

How grand is such an action
In this full world of strife!
Such deeds are deeply graven
Within the Book of Life:
And coming years should honour
The noble miner's name
In metal and in marble
With everlasting fame.

Lines In My Own Life
by John Harris

ON the quiet evening of October 14th, 1820, in a straw-thatched, boulder-built cottage, with bare rafters and clay floor, locally known as the Six Chimneys, on the top of Bolenowe Hill, Camborne, Cornwall, as the leaves are falling from the trees, and the robin mourns in the thicket, a gentle mother gives birth to a babe; and that baby-boy is a poet. The little fellow is just like other children, and grows up so much like his compeers that he attracts but slender notice above the young bipeds around him. He cries for things he ought not to cry for, gives his mother not a little trouble by poking his fingers into bits forbidden, has his wheelbarrow, cart and spade, and soon grows vain of his buttoned dress and cap with waving plume. Very early in life, what time the red sun sinks behind the purple hills, and the first bright stars look through the firmament, he is taught to kneel at his bed-side, and repeat, 'Our Father.' And then come picture-books and toys, marbles and trundling-hoops, and anon Little Red Riding Hood, Goody Two Shoes, Jack the Giant Killer, Sally Meanwell, Fifth of November, and then the green satchel, and away to the village school. See him sitting on the end of a low stool, when not much more than five years of age, and taught by an old Cornish crone the letters of the alphabet. Slowly, slowly, the crooked characters find a lodgement in his memory, and swim before his eyes. At length he masters the hornbook, and takes his place on an upper seat. His father and his mother praise his proficiency; and he leaves the learned village schoolmistress, and is placed under an iron master. This man is exceedingly hard-hearted and cruel, and verily hoots the lessons in his ears. He beats his pupils without mercy, with a polished piece of flat wood, studded with small sharp nails, until the blood runs down, and soon scares the little learner from his straw-roofed academy. Nor must the Wesleyan Sunday-school in the hamlet be forgotten, where he hears with glad heart 'the story of the Cross,' in which he remains for more than thirty years, and the religious teaching therein received tinctures all his future life.

On the edge of a brown common, in a little thatched school-house by the side of the highway, very near the famous Nine Maidens, he finds another master, who wore a wooden leg, with more of the milk of human kindness in his soul, a thorough Christian, and a man of much prayer. Here he plods through the spelling-book, and walks like a conqueror into the mazes of arithmetic, learns to read and write, leaving all other branches of knowledge to slumber in forgetfulness. The evenings of his boyhood are evenings of purest joy. Sitting by the old hearth-stone where his grandfather had sat before him, and another generation had mused and passed away – sitting by the old hearth-stone, and gazing up in his mother's face, he listens to her wild stories with wondering joy. She tells of sorrow and weeping as the lot of all, and of Him who came to redeem the world. The tears will often start into his eyes, and a gentle spirit whispers in the cells of his soul. And now, cowering by the old grate, in the dim fire-light which clothes the walls in shadowy warriors and plumed knights mounted on floating steeds, and a thousand nameless fantastic shapes, he hangs over the *Pilgrim's Progress*, a tattered volume of doggerel rhyme, written by an old scarred soldier, and *Cook's Voyages round the World*. Then come a few stray notes from the mystic lyre of the undying Burns, in an old time eaten copy of the *Cotter's Saturday Night*, found among a few antique books belonging to his father; and its tuneful echoes float through the chambers of his soul like breathings from an AEolian harp, and ever haunt him in the silence of his reedy cot. You might have seen him on a summer evening, when his merry schoolmates are chattering in the hollow, – you might have seen him walking by the stream, or stretched on the moss, listening to the wind tuning its organ among the rocks, or gazing up at the purple heavens. He roams among the flowers, kissing them for very joy, calling them his fragrant sisters. Born on the crest of the hill, amid the crags and storms, he grows up in love with Nature, and she becomes his chief teacher. And now come the first promptings of early genius which develop themselves in snatches of unpolished song, pencilled on the leaves of his copy-book for the amusement of his wondering schoolmates. He often writes his rhymes on the clean side of cast-off labelled tea-papers which his mother brings from the shop, and then reads them to his astonished compeers with rapt delight. At the age of nine comes the great monster combat, his struggle for daily bread, when he is taken off from school, and put to work in the fields. At the age of ten he is employed by an old tin-streamer in the moor to throw the white sand from the river, earning the odd sum of three pence per day. O my countrymen, ye little think how many burning and shining lights ye extinguish in life's aspiring morning for want of a helping hand! O my countrymen, tread not upon the errand-boy with music in his heart, or the ploughman's son who draws fresh pictures of his father's sheep, or the little slimy miner with his model engine, the work of his fruitful brain; tread not upon the poor child of genius, do not freeze his soul with the frigid fingers of neglect, but cheer him with your kindness and warm him with your smile; so shall the great world be made holier and happier by your existence, and learn to bless your name!

At the early age of twelve years we find him in the mine working on the surface nearly three miles from his favourite home. As he travels to and from his labour through long lanes bramble-covered, and over meadows snowy with daisies, or by hedges blue with hyacinths, or over whispering cairns redolent with the hum of bees, the beautiful world around him teems with syllables of song. Even then he pencils his strange ditties reciting them at intervals of leisure to the dwellers of his own district, and older heads than his tell of his future fame. When thirteen summers have filled his lap with roses and fanned his forehead with the breeze of health, we find him sweating in the hot air of the interior of a mine* working with his father nearly two hundred fathoms below the green fields. Morning and evening he has to descend and ascend the ladders, for there was no man-engine in those days, so that his flannel dress is often wet with perspiration, like the locks of the hills with rain. But a gentle lay is ever ringing in his ears, and the angel of hope is brooding over his path. Now he writes a copy of verses for a poor blind man, and listens ashamed behind a bookstall as the sightless miner sings them in the streets.

On rushes the great world in the pursuit of mammon, little heeding the boy-bard in his zone of numbers, the composition of whose untutored melodies brings rich reward to his own heart. He is told that if he continues to invoke the song-spirit and write poetry, he must forgo gold and silver, houses and lands, eat the bread of carefulness, live, perhaps, in a hovel, and die at last on a pallet of straw. But in spite of this unreasonable picture, he works away at his barrel-organ during his leisure moments, which is as dear to him as his own life.

Though the great God placed the lyre in his hands, and poetry appeared to him to be his greatest work in the world, yet he feels that for it he must not neglect his allotted labours, but pursue the path in which Providence has placed him, believing that to act thus would be noble and manly, not depending on literature as a means of pecuniary support, but partaking it as a pleasurable relaxation amid the cares of life.

And thus he travels on through the vale of boyhood, labouring with his hands, and singing with his soul, as solitary as a stranger among his own people, without a single friend to direct him; for how is it possible to educate the poet? What means can you devise to burnish his golden

* *Dolcoth, Camborne, Cornwall.*

fancies that span the universe like belts of shining jasper? Try, if you please, with the chisel of art; but it will only be a fatal mistake. "The only way to educate the poet is to honour him." *

On plods the young minstrel of the mountain, kneeling at the shrine of Nature, taught only by her look and voice. Whilst those of his own age and acquaintance spend their leisure in merry companionship, wasting the hour in song and wassail, he is roaming with the echoes, brushing the dew-drops from the flowers. Wherever he goes, he takes his sacred harp: and whether he is in his father's field, turning up the sod with his spade, or guiding the plough along the furrow, whether he is in the shop or the shed, the mine or the mart, there is ever one object before him, and that object is his verse writing. It grows with his physical growth, and is dearer to him than the smile of friendship. See him in his dear old chimney-nook, with paper and pencil on his knee, writing rhymes by the firelight, while his buxom brothers are shouting like tempests around him. And this is his only study, save the barn or the cow-house. He sometimes pencils his poems in the grey light of morning on the white-washed walls of his bed-room, while all the other members of his father's family are asleep. How does he long, on some cold winter evening, when the cottage inmates are all garrulous around him, thundering the village gossip at the same moment, dinning his ears as he sits with pale face wooing the Muse among them, – how does he long for some obscure corner, where, with a handful of fire in the grate, and a small lamp upon the unplaned board, he could write his songs in quiet! But this is denied him, and so the hills and valleys, woods and wolds, are his favourite haunts for composition, amid the lonely ruin or by the naked rock; often in cold weather composing his pieces walking up and down the fields, or over the moors, or sitting in his bedroom, with his feet wrapped in his mother's cloak, a pair of small bellows for his writing desk.

And in the brown autumn-time, when a pensive calm pervades the woods, and a solemn rustle is heard upon the hills, he makes ink to write his idylls with the juice of blackberries which grow on the hedges of his mountain-meads. He saves the pence given him in the holidays by his father and his friends, and lays them out in the purchase of books; and the neighbours are also kind in lending him any new numbers from their shelves. But his own stock is very limited; and when he has access to the

* The Spirit of German Poetry *by Joseph Gostick*

Sunday-school library in the village, he rejoices with great joy. Are there days of rain and storm, or drizzling mist, which are often, as holidays, weariness and misery to many? They are gilt with glory for him; for in some "cell confined" he is at his song-grinding as happy as a monarch, while visions of beauty crowd upon his soul.

Love meets him on his flowery pathway, and he weaves a chaplet of the choicest roses to adorn her brow. He worships at the shrine of beauty till they stand before the sacred altar, and the two are made one. The world is now filled with sunshine, life's cup overflows with bliss, and he walks over the earth as through a paradise. Still he pursues his verse-writing, till a short lyric "To the Robin" finds its way into the pages of a Magazine, and his heart throbs with delight as those well conned lines of his are first immortalized in printer's ink, He struggles with adversity as with a giant; and day after day, and often night after night, finds him in the smoky eaves of the deep mine.

Here his labours are most exhausting, often from morning till night, and from night till morning, far below the light of day, or sun, or moon, or star, with those who have but little love for his song-seraph, –

> Blasting the rude earth,
> Which fell with such a crash, that he who heard
> Cried, "Jesu, save the miner!"

But she cheered his heart in the sulphur, and sang among the fiery flints, robbing the severest labour of half its blight. Many times has he escaped sudden death, almost by miracle, from masses of falling earth, or the sudden blasting of the rock. Watch him as he walks at morning to his daily toil. He seeks not the company of those who may be travelling on the same road, but more enjoys himself alone. Not a moment passes unimproved. He turns over the numbers of some unfinished poem, polishing the periods as best he may, weighing the words and smoothing the ringing euphony. Ever and anon he seeks for an opportunity, when no eye beholds him, and inscribes his verses with a worn pencil on a piece of waste paper he carries in his pocket. Often, to hide it from the passer-by, he lets it slip up in his coat-sleeve, holding it with his fingers. The new thought preserved, he hastens to his labour filled with bright designs. In the midst of his toil his fancy is revelling with song, leading him among crystal fountains and bowers of living green. He sometimes writes lines of poetry on his thumb-nails, often on pieces of roof-slate and shreds of common tile, sometimes on the insides and crown of his hat, and on iron wedges down deep in the hollowed earth. Is there a secret path leading to his home? He is sure at evening to be found in it, holding strange conversation with the flowers, or shapes invisible. Often does he cower behind a hedge till his comrades have passed him, so that in silence and solitude he may finish his lay. And how they have stared sometimes, clustered under the hawthorn to hear him recite his ditties in the summer moonlight, praising the uneducated author! Has he an hour's leisure and cessation from manual labour, that hour is spent with the Muses; and whilst others of his own calling waste their time in rambling the streets, or roaming the lanes in idle and unprofitable chit-chat, or ruining body and soul in those dark drinking-dens which frown like famines over the land, he steals away to his bower of heath with his harp upon his shoulder, intent on his one object. His company is but little courted by the chatting choir; for in conversation he is remarkably stupid, scarcely ever uttering the right word; so that what was said of poor Goldsmith in this respect is truly applicable to him.

Time passes on; Providence blesses him with children, and domestic cares increase; but he still sweeps his fingers over his harp, and the Muse is to him a solace and a joy. And now a kind friend* steps across his path, whose honoured name is syllabled by the great and good of many lands, and aids him in his up-hill course, and a small volume of his poems passes through the press. This volume wins for him the warm sympathies of many hearts, and he again betakes him to his studies with sunshine in his soul. Let us look in upon him at evening in his own loved home, when his daily task is done, and he has just returned from the hard drudgery of the interior of the mine, exhausted and cruelly crushed. A few worn books are piled up in a comer on some narrow shelves, and three of the most conspicuous are, Walker's Dictionary, sweet Burns, and the immortal Shakespeare. We must not omit his Bible, the gift of his sainted father, the sweet stories of which so charmed him when a boy. Scraps of paper, written over with jingling rhyme, lie among the volumes, and sleep in quiet nooks, jotted by his own hand. A small fire is burning in the stove; on one side of it sits his wife, plying her needle with a smile upon her face; a bright girl, with soft poetic eyes, is conning her lesson at his feet; and a blue-eyed boy, like a laughing Cupid, is climbing his knees and kissing his pale brow. The weary poet, crushed and crippled with the labours of the day, lets fall a tear upon the cheek of his little one, returns its sweet caress, and for a season forgets his lassitude as he gazes into the fire, where a thousand strange shapes flit to and fro. He shares his frugal meal with his dear ones, and blesses God for what they enjoy. And now he tells the children their wanted story, joins them in their sports, dances baby in his arms, or writes his poetry as they crow upon his knees. O, sweet is his domestic bliss, and bright angels are bending over the walls of glory to gaze upon the scene.

* *Dr. G. Smith, author of* History of Wesleyan Methodism.

"He owns neither mansions nor lands,
His wealth is a character good,
A pair of industrious hands,
A drop of poetical blood.

He never of fortune complains,
Of parentage, learning, or birth;
The sweat of his brow, and his brains,
Yield more than he asketh on earth.

His bliss are his eventide hours;
His book, wife, and children, his pride;
In joy they're his sweetest of flowers,
And angels when sorrows betide."

Edward Capern

And when at last his cottage roses fall asleep, and fold themselves in beauty, and quiet is brooding over his shed, it is then that his verses are written, and his thoughts twined into rhyme. But chief he loves to be away from the dwellings of men, with rocks and rills and flowers, poetizing in the shadowy twilight. Here he feels a purer inspiration, and revels through lands enchanted. He woos the Muse as a lover his mistress, seeking some flowery bank in the bosom of solitude, and here he pens his poems,

"Where Nature sows, herself,
And reaps her crops; whose garments are the clouds;
Whose minstrels, brooks; whose lamps, the moon and stars;
Whose organ-choir, the voice of many waters;
Whose banquets, morning dews; whose heroes, storms;
Whose warriors, mighty winds; whose lovers, flowers;
Whose orators, the thunderbolts of God;
Whose palaces, the everlasting hills;
Whose ceiling, heaven's unfathomable blue;
And from whose rocky turrets, battled high,
Prospects immense spread out on all sides round,
Lost now between the welkin and the main,
Now wall'd with hills that sleep above the storm."

Pollok

In his work and in his home, by the wayside and on the pathless wild, in the dusty street and on the sand of the sea-shore, there is evermore this gentle spirit beside him, cheering life's weary pilgrimage, and alluring him onward in spite of ten thousand difficulties. As it was when he first found his lyre, amid the ferns of his father's fens, even so it is now, when pursuing his solemn labours among the aged and afflicted – a sunny joy and an unceasing solace cheering him at all seasons, and under all skies; with his rising family, and limited salary. Thus he pursues his even course; rarely indulging in the reading of a book, drinking at the rills of Nature, singing by his hearth-stone and amid the silent solitudes, not neglecting for it one social or domestic duty, tracing the hand of God in everything. He would not omit a kind word for his patrons and friends, who have aided him in his up-hill course, and cheered his journey over the desert of life, invoking the blessing of the great King upon them.

He knows that knowledge is not acquired through the medium of the wishing-cap, nor genius by the wand of the enchantress. If we desire to be useful to our fellow-creatures, and distinguish ourselves above the careless crowd around us, it must be accomplished by diligent labour and perseverance in the right direction. We should not be discouraged by unpromising surroundings, recalling to mind the brave and brilliant host who have toiled through the valley of labour, oppressed with weariness and pain; but whose flaming souls bore them far above the rough rubbish of the rude world, until the green laurel was placed upon their brows. He remembers that beautiful allegorical poem of Longfellow, the great American poet, in which he describes a young man wandering among the mountains of the Alps, bearing in his hand a banner, upon which is written this strange device, "Excelsior." This young man is represented by the poet as beginning to climb one of those mighty mountains, on whose crest is eternal winter, bearing this strange banner in his hand; when he is met by a peasant, who endeavours to dissuade him from the task. But he glances at the banner, "Higher, and yet higher still," and, leaving the peasant behind him, he hastens on his way. Farther up, on the rough ridges of the kingly mount, he meets with another traveller, who tries to discourage him, and persuade him to go back. But once more he gazes at the banner, "Higher, and yet higher still," and with eager footsteps he climbs towards the stars. Higher, and yet higher still, the young man climbs, bearing his banner aloft from crag to slippery crag, from white snow-field to snow-field, higher and higher from this wicked world, till a wanderer, wending through the snow, finds him lying in the winds, with the mark of death upon his forehead, still grasping the banner in his icy hand, and over him, high up in the blue fields of ether, a spirit is singing sweetly – 'tis the spirit of the youth still chanting the word, "Excelsior." To the young especially we would say, Emblazon the word "Excelsior" on your banner, "higher, and yet higher still." Go forth with it into the world, act under its dictates, and circumstances shall bend before you. Aim at a certain object, turn your steps towards it perseveringly, hopefully, cheerfully; and, by and by, we pledge ourselves you shall be crowned with the laurel. Christian! emblazon the word "Excelsior" on thy banner, "higher, and yet higher still." Heed not those who would entice thee to go back; keep thine eye on the crown before thee, walk in the footprints of the blessed Redeemer; rear aloft thy standard, "Higher, and yet higher still," and soon the ivory palaces of heaven will be thy home. Let us take this motto as our burning, living watchword, "Higher, and yet higher still," higher in Christian experience, higher in the knowledge of God, higher in the Divine life, higher in the scale of existence, higher in acts of benevolence, and deeds of good-will toward our fellow-creatures; "higher, and yet higher still," till we climb the green hills of Eden, and gather flowers in the fields of light.

Extract from:-
'Her Husband was a Miner'

Her husband was a miner, toiling where
The light of morning never found its way,
Or star-beam gilt the gloom; where night remain'd,
Blacker than Boreas when he hides the hills,
And shrouds the valleys with his dismal wings.
His eldest boy strove with him, twelve springs old;
A bud in shade, a blossom in the dark.
And they were wont the ladders to descend,
Tied in a rope. At one end was his sire
Going down before, and after him the lad
Came clinging to the staves. Around their waists
The cord was fasten'd; so that, if the child
Fell, he might save him as he downward dropp'd,

And bring him to his mother and his home.
He was a tributer; a man who work'd
On speculation, digging through the ground
In search of ore, the sweetener of his toil.
If found, he flourish'd; if not found, he fell;
Nor fell alone, fell wife and family.

But much misery was he doom'd to feel.
Long months of disappointment, nights of woe,
And days of strife, and mental agony:
He dug, and found not; dug and dug again,
Again to be the loser – all was dead.
He ventured till his clothes were heavy rags,
And the last shilling glided from his purse.
Yet hope sang with him in the sulphur-rifts,
And pictured bright to-morrows. And when green
Tinctured the rock, or copper stain'd the stone,
In fancy he beheld his stores increase,
His pile of mineral levell'd on the floors,
His debts discharged, his wife in new attire,
His houshold songsters warmly clothed and fed,
His new home rising by the running brook,
His farm enclosed, his pretty meadows till'd,
Poultry and pigs rejoicing in the stye,
and Molly 'neath the hawthorn by the gate
Chewing her cud in quiet. So he dug,
With eyes the home of tears, and heart in heaven:
But when men elbow'd him along the street,
And frown'd upon him in his patch'd-up vest,
And cries of hunger echoed in his home,
His heart sank in him, and the angel Hope
For a short season travell'd from his side.

ESSAY 1

THE LAND'S END (A letter to E.B.)

Land's End,
Thursday, August 28, 1856.

WELL, here we are in a fog-shroud, groping our way around the Logan Rock, and shivering amidst the grandeur of the Land's End: mist, mist, nothing but mist! I declare I was quite angry with the fog-sprite; for, from the first moment we entered on this wild array of crags, to the time I am now pencilling these lines in "First and Last," (the name of the inn at the Land's End,) this invisible tormentor has been sputtering away till we are quite drenched through to the skin.

I think the Land's End to be the most sublime thing I have ever seen in nature. How the dark waves dash against those rocks, and foam and hiss, moaning hoarse tales of storms, and shipwrecks, and callous wreckers in days of old! Everlastingly they come and go, thumping the walls of the old cliff with giant fury, and then recoiling in jets of foam! And the light-house in the midst of the waters, and the sea-birds on the ledges of the rocks, or floating over the waves, or chiming to the hoarse bass of the billows, as they dash through the sparry grottoes, – all conspire to endear it to the memory of the bard.

But the mist is still falling, or rather driving. We are hastening back over the moor, fragrant with flowers, to our nest for the night, ever and anon pulling off a tuft of heather, and asking questions of our cheerful guide, who seems to tell us all he knows. And now the old clock on the top of the stairs is striking eight, Jane is almost exhausted with the day's long journey, and for the *first time in my life* I retire to rest away from home. So good night until the morning.

Friday morning, August 29th. The old clock struck ten, eleven, and still I slept not. The little white chamber seemed full of wicked elves, which prided themselves on keeping my eyelids open. The moan of the old ocean came up on the blast, which hurried over the house-top with a furious twitch; and a couple of fat travellers in an adjoining room kept whistling and singing; so that I wished them somewhere else. I never expected to get into dream-land or sleep-land, and was just about to leap out of bed, and commence an angry poem, or rush down to the wild beach and listen to the midnight songs of the sea, when sweet sleep fell on me like a beautiful spell.

When I awoke, the winds were hushed, the mist was gone, the light of the morning was streaming through the window, the sea-birds were wheeling over the heaths, a robin sang under the eaves of the old inn, and the light-house was shining like an angel in the midst of the waters. So away we went in the matin breezes, down, down past Johnson's Head, away on the extreme crags of the Land's End; and, O, what a wilderness of wonders was there! We felt doubly paid for the mist, doubly paid for our long walk, as the huge clouds rolled back from the rising sun, and the great sea became bluer and bluer, and the Scilly Islands rose up to view, and the noisy gulls called to each other in the crevices of the cliff, or cried upon the waters like poets of the billows.

I stood upon one of the crags and repeated Charles Wesley's hymn, and felt I had begun a new era in my existence. Why, the Land's End is like a great craggy poem, epic or otherwise. Every poet should read it, and make it his own. Thanks to you for directing me there.

ESSAY 2

BOOK MAKING

"OF making many books there is no end." Man has invented a thousand things to immortalize his name, and hand it down to posterity. Mausoleums are built, monuments are raised, the brass is engraven, and pyramids tower up to heaven, which seem to defy the tooth of Time, and laugh at the world's destroyer. But mausoleums crumble into ruins, pyramids are dashed to the earth, monuments are ground into powder and scattered on the four winds of heaven, and

"The busto moulders and the brass consumes."

Words written in books are the only things that live on, surviving the desolations of age, only to fall amid

"The wreck of matter and the crush of worlds."

Hence, in all ages and in all countries, multitudes have been, and still are, devoting all their energies and all their powers to the composition and publication of books.

O what a cloudy age was that, ere the art of printing was known, when our rough fathers, for want of better materials, and for want of wiser heads, used to write and make books on the leaves and bark of trees and square blocks of wood! Time passed away, paper was invented, the art of printing was known, and thought flashed forth in graceful columns like a thing of magic life. But, for a long period, the price of a Bible was so high, that it was chiefly confined to the clergy and the nobility. Now it ornaments the towns and beautifies the villages of almost all lands. It smiles in the valley, and shines among the crags of the mountain; it pours forth its solemn music under the trees of the hamlet, and amid the heather of the wild; beside the rural hedge-row and the dusty highway. The worthy colporteur drops them by river and by rock, by fountain and by fen, in forest and in field, by snow-heap and in summer bower; so that, from zone to zone, they smile like guardian angels amid the moral waste.

The writer of the words at the head of our essay was a wise man and a rich, so that his fame had gone forth into all the world. Monarchy came down from its throne, and crossed valleys and mountains, to hear his wisdom and to gaze upon his wealth. His eyes roamed among the trees of the forest, where the axe of the woodman had never been heard; and he spake of them all from the cedar that is in Lebanon, to the hyssop that springeth out of the wall. He spake of beasts that fatten in the forest, or revel in the wilderness, or roam through the solitudes of the boundless desert. He scanned the fields of air, and sang of birds with starry wings, which float through the groves like the bright imagery of the bards, or carol on the branches of the palm-trees in the shadowy twilight to sing the fair daughters of the young world asleep. He spake of creeping things that inhabit the earth, sheltering in mountains and valleys, or existing in the crevices of the rocks, or hiding among the grasses of the glen, or burrowing in the slimy mould. He gazed upon the sea, blue and beautiful, boundless and benign, rolling its thunders on the rocky strand, or flowing in billows of rich music on the listening shore. And he spake of fishes great, and fishes small; of fishes that float on its mighty surface, or those that hide in its fathomless grottoes. Thus he spake of the earth, the sea, and the sky, and almost all that is therein. He had, too, a deep knowledge of nature and the human heart, and uttered three thousand proverbs for the profit of man. He snatched his harp, and the Muse came to his aid, and his proverbial philosophy has descended to us in rich strains of song. Lyric after lyric was added to his list, until they numbered a thousand and five. But after an age of experience, after labouring and accumulating so much, after acquiring and accomplishing more than any man in his day, he comes to this conclusion, "Of making many books there is no end."

As it was in the days of king Solomon, so it is now during the reign of our beloved widowed Queen; of making many books there is still no end. The historian sits him down and ransacks old musty volumes, and by their aid he gazes upon buried cities and countries desolate. He rushes over the war-field, and hears the neigh of the battle-horse, as it dashes to the fray. He traces the rise and fall of empires, and lays proud kings in their tombs. He revels with the shadows of the past, and lifts off the shroud from the urn of the destroyer. He spends a whole lifetime in studious retirement, and then gathers up his thoughts and binds them in a book. The astronomer directs his telescope to the stars, and walks among them in the shroud of night. He converses with the constellations, and calls the planets by their names. System after system is added to his list, and the mysteries of creation are revealed by his researches. He, too, culls his wonderful discoveries, and binds them in a book. The geologist racks his brains, and tortures his imagination, to arrive at new theories, how the mountains were created, and the hills brought forth; how the rocks are above ground and under ground; how earthquakes rend the globe, and volcanoes belch forth flame. His thoughts, too, are gathered up, and bound into a book. The poet seeks the shades of solitude, shuns the haunts of men, and hides him in the glens and lichened caves. He wanders by the sea-shore, and hears strange music in the murmur of the billows.

He finds:-

"Tongues in the trees, books in the running streams,
    Sermons in stones, and good in everything."

He robes the earth in beauty, flinging strange spells over the hills and valleys. He weaves the cobwebs of rural life into silken flowers, to beautify the homes of his fatherland. He, too, gathers up his musings, and binds them in a book. But the historian, the astronomer, the geologist, and the poet die, and fade away like the mists of morning; and we come to the conclusion that he alone is wise who loves his Saviour, and whose name is written in the Lamb's book of life. This book will stand when all other books are destroyed and burnt together at Nature's funeral pile.

THE MINE
Part 1

Home from his pit among the reeds and flags,
Where he had dug for months, and dug in vain,
The pale man came to dinner. Lost in thought,
Upon a bench, at the low table's end,
He ate his barley pasty *minus* meat,
Stuff'd with potatoes and enough of salt.
His lean dog watch'd him by the three-legg'd stool,
And in a cage beside his lattice small
An old thrush chatter'd with a marvellous glee.
His wife, her face upon her wasted hands,
Sat in the chimney by the red peat fire,
Watching the smoke ascend, the smutty stack,
And lost meanwhile in wondrous reverie.
Laying his knife upon the wooden plate,
He broke the silence with a heavy sigh :-
"'t is no use, Maggie, digging any more.
I've ventured till we've only one goat left,
The weakest of the flock: the kids are gone,
And all the sheep and lambs have long been sold:
The cows have vanish'd from the untill'd fields,
And all the horses have been driven away,
Save that poor pony, lean, you see, and long:
The pigs and poultry feed in other yards,
And every sack of corn has left the barn.
I sold the straw last night to farmer Jones,
And neighbour Lambrick bought the rick of hay.
Not a potato in the outhouse lies:
The furze is taken from the under croft,
And all the turf is carried from Beck's carne.
My bran-best hat and breeches waterproof,
My buckled boots, my best, my yellow-topp'd,
Bridle and saddle, and my darling cane,
With silver head and silver studded o'er,
I bought when we were married, – all are gone,
And I am left alone, a ruin'd man.
Dame, look around you: where the chest of drawers?
Where all the pewter? where the copper pans?
Where the old china, rich indeed for age,

The bright tin teapots, and the oaken chairs?
Gone! and the crack'd panes echo, 'Gone!'
I've work'd until my bones are almost bare,
And Hope has shrieking left me; and, to fill
This dark-hued cup to overflowing quite,
Our only boy could bear distress no more,
And so last night he left us for the seas.
O God, have mercy on us and the lad!"

The poor man groan'd and shook his streaming locks.
Resting his back against the cupboard door,
He fix'd his eyes upon an empty shelf.
Then Maggie's full heart pour'd its treasures forth.
She told of many men of humble birth
Who persevered in duty's upward path,
And won estates, rich fortunes, and a name.
"Last night," she said, "I dreamt 'twas summer-time,
And we were walking by a limpid lake,
Whose face was crystal as the mirror'd heavens,
And overhead the tall trees shadow'd us,
And shook their leaves with gladness. We sat down,
And listen'd to the birds, and mark'd the kine
Feeding upon the lawn, while round us lay
Orchards of fruit and fields of waving corn;
And all was ours, and all the gift of Heaven.
But I awoke, and, lo, it was a dream."
And then she bade him not to be dismay'd,
But trust in God, who made the mighty hills,
And placed the minerals in their hidden cells;
That nothing came of him who ceased to act,
And wept at every steep he had to climb.
The navigator, hoping against hope,
Still steer'd his vessel over darksome seas,
Until new lands were added to his chart.
The general led his armies on and on,
Through days and nights of fever and fatigue,
Until the city sank beneath his tread.
So he should never give despair a place,
But go and try again another week. –
That week brought fortune in a mine of wealth.

It happen'd thus. Down from a distant carne
An old man came, with wisdom in his face;

Mean his attire, and homely was his speech,
But warm his heart that beat beneath a frieze;
And calling at the tinner's rustic door.
The following morn, he gently knock'd, and said,
"Cheer up, faint heart : I'm come to give thee aid."
And forth upon the moor of pits they went,
Conversing by the way of lodes and veins.
Meanwhile a cloud went marching up the sky,
And blacker grew and blacker, mounting higher,
Until it reel'd and stagger'd o'er their heads,
And sent forth streams of fire that roll'd along
The rocky valley like a flaming beast.
The two men gazed, and cloud and fire were gone.
Then much they chatted in the light of morn.

Spoke the old man with warm heart wrapp'd in frieze,
"This is the dragon of the mineral vault:
He's out but rarely, and his presence shows
A mine of riches wheresoe'er he rolls.
His track was down the sheep-path by the oak,
Where hung for months the miser suicide.
Strange sounds wail through the branches in dark night,
Or when the winds are high or breezes low.
Howbeit, near the oak the dragon roll'd,
Close by the pit where you were digging last,
Sad and discouraged. But this augurs well
For you, my neighbour: and we'll try once more
What virtue's in the famous dowzing-rod."
So from a white thorn, with his large clasp-knife,
The old man cut a twig formed like a V,
And, holding it in both his oozy hands
Point uppermost, he paced along the vale
From north to south, till, near the hangman-oak,
The point turn'd downwards with a sudden twitch,
And rays of joy shot from the old man's eyes.
Then back he went, and forth he came again,
Holding the rod in both his oozy hands,
And down it went over the same mark'd spot.
So he was satisfied, and said, "Sink here:
There is a mineral-chamber underneath
Will well repay you for your little loss.
Behind yon mount o'er which the sun has climb'd

They saw a fire like this: I used the rod,
And where it turn'd, two labourers sank a pit,
Who now have coaches, titles, and estates.
I'll wager, sinking here, you'll have a mine."
And o'er the hills the dowzer pass'd away.

The vale is silent, silent are the trees,
And still the waters of the sleeping lake:
The lark's last note has floated up to heaven,
And down the stream the merry boatman glides,
And louder sings as drawing nearer home.
The smoke is curling upwards o'er the pines,
And merry voices ring among the flowers,
As Eve reposes on a primrose bank.
Amid the reeds a gentle damsel sighs
Like harper in the thicket, and the wren
Puts out his ear among the springing ferns,
To listen to the sorrows of the maid.
"He's gone, he's gone, my loving Henry's gone:
To-day we parted by the village gate,
What time the sun had reach'd his highest noon.
He shook my hand, and tears came in his eyes;
And seeing his, mine own were dim with rain;
And when he told me he should sail away
Across the ocean to a land of heat,
And seek his fortune in a grot of gold,
Because his father with a hero's heart
Lost all his little digging for a mine,
My heart seem'd bursting in me, and I thought
I should have sunk upon the flinty ground.

"Don't weep," he murmur'd; "when a few short years
Have pass'd like visions, Henry will return,
When the church bells shall ring our wedding chime,
And we be one and happy. Far away,
Alone with strangers and a selfish world,
Thine image shall be with me, going out
And coming in, and sitting by my chair,
And mirror'd on the universe of light.
I'll wear thee vision'd on my heart of hearts;
And when the daylight dies among the hills,
And Eve steals onward with her urn of dews,
I'll think I see thee by thy cottage door,
And hear thy song float o'er the listening trees,

And feel thou prayest for thy Henry gone.'
He kiss'd my hand, and soon was out of sight."

In a rude land he labour'd with success,
Till one bright morn beneath an ancient tree
A group of men are standing. Some have rings,
And some have purses, little boxes some;
And some have letters cramm'd with lines of love;
And some have bits of gold, and some have coin;
And some have strings of pearl, and some have shells;
And some have portraits of their household flowers,
Loved, happy faces, group'd in miniature;
And some have books, and some have curls of hair,
And ribbons some, and some have metal pens,
And some have landscapes lengthen'd on a leaf,
And some have little poems wet with tears.
All eyes are bent upon a fair young man,
With staff in hand and bundle on his back,
And face towards his home in Cornish-land;
And these are trifles for their distant friends,
Child, mother, wife, and lover: so he placed
Each tiny treasure in his travelling-bag,
Shook hands with all, and hasten'd on his way.

Return we to the tinner of the moor.
Soon as the dowzer left him, he went home,
And made his breakfast off a crust of bread
With salt and water on the great hearth warm'd;
And then he took his pickaxe, pipe, and spade,
And ancient canteen swinging in his hand,
And down the sheep-path once more travell'd he
Into the place of pits, a hopeful man.
Laying aside his outer vest, his eyes
Instinctively turn'd upwards, and he sigh'd,
"O Father, if it be Thy holy will,
Prosper the labour of Thy servant's hands.
The gold is Thine, the tin and copper Thine:
Direct me where to labour with success.
However, not my will, but Thine be done."
And down into the earth the pickaxe went,
As if a giant dash'd it in the ground.

Down went his shaft through various strata-crusts,
Thick layer after layer, till he came

Upon a hope-reviving bed of blue.
He brought up samples with a gladden'd heart,
And wash'd them in the rill among the reeds,
And they produced some grains of real tin.
Next day a boy came with him, and they placed
A windlass on the shaft, and wound the stuff
Up in a goatskin fashion'd like a bag.
Each day the lode grew richer, and more tin
Was lying on the surface. Then he made
A wooden wheel, and placed it in the moor,
And on some stakes of oak put iron heads,
To stamp the rough stones into powder fine.
Then o'er the wheel he turn'd the limpid stream,
And round it went; up rose the heavy heads,
And falling bruised the stones to mineral sand.
So cleaning it, the old man's pony bore
The treasure to the far-off smelting-house;
And he return'd with twenty pounds or more.
And as it chimed within his mole-skin purse,
How Maggie's bright eyes twinkled with delight!
That eve a grateful prayer rose up to heaven.

Then weeks and months and seasons pass'd away,
And tin was wound up in the goatskin bag,
And clean'd, and carried to the smelting-house;
And he return'd with guineas in his purse;
Till one still eve he sat upon his bench
Much pondering. Leaping quickly up, he said,
"I have a whim now whirling in my pate:
I'll work it out to-morrow." When day dawn'd,
And to the covert slunk the full-fed fox,
He cut down wood and nail'd it like a cage
With horizontal slabs and slabs oblique,
And through the centre a rough forest tree
Placed for an axle, and from out its side
Ran two arms like a giant's. Near the shaft
He set it up, and round it twined a rope,
Brought o'er a pulley by the tin-pit's mouth;
And to the rope a wooden barrel swung,
Made by a cooper in his village shop.
He harness'd pony to the great wood arm,
And round and round and round again it went,
Pulling the barrel up and down the shaft,

Till heaps of tin upon the surface lay,
And Fortune fill'd his mole-skin purse with gold.
And seasons came and pass'd, and came again;
Rains fell, and sunshine kiss'd the gladden'd earth;
The crops grew up and fell before the scythe;
Men woo'd and married, feasted, fail'd, and died.
Levels were driven, and other shafts were sunk;
An adit from a valley drain'd the mine;
Great heaps of tin upon the surface lay,
And still went round the whim and waterwheel.

There dwelt among the hills a thoughtful boy,
Whose mother was the model of her sex;
And he was very forward for his years,
Fond of good books and study. Other lads
Seem'd only happy when engaged in play;
He when with God and nature. On a time,
As he sat musing by his cottage-grate,
The boiling kettle hiss'd upon the hearth,
And so he stopp'd the steam and stirr'd the fire,
His mother looking on with chiding eyes, –
Until the power confined thrust out itself,
And burst the kettle in its rage for fame.
This led the student on to higher things,
From steep to dizzy steep, until at last
He made the great steam-engine, when the world
Received a boon to bless it evermore.
And so Watt's name is carved among the great,
And chimed in song, and deck'd with summer flowers.

Meanwhile the mine extended and grew rich,
And every month the workmen multiplied;
The water gush'd from countless cracks unseen,
Ran down the levels' sides, and bubbled up
Within the adit, keeping the bold men
From sinking far beneath it, till the wheel
Was laid aside, and in its place arose
A small steam-engine newly wonderful;
And wonderful the ease with which it wrought,
Draining the mine as strangely as a spell.
After the shaft was sixty feet in depth,
Ends were extended eastward, westward far;
Then winzes sunk for air from level to level;
And so it ever was and ever is.
And as they sunk from rugged stair to stair,

The troubled entrails of the rifled world
Changed hard as marble. Drills were introduced,
And mallets rang where picks had clink'd before.
Then holes were blasted in a dangerous way,
    By rushes thrust into the powder-charge
Through a small hole made by a copper wire,
    Igniting it as sudden as a thought;
Ere the poor wretch could say one word of prayer,
    Destroying limbs and often life itself.
Then quills were used. Still very dangerous they
    And more expensive. Turn we from the fields,
    And ladder after ladder quick descend,
    Until we reach a labourer's working-place.
    It is the hour of morning: on a plank
    A father and his elder son sit down,
    A boy with fourteen Aprils on his face,
With thought of home and brothers in his mind,
And sunny slopes and lawns of laughing flowers,
    Denied him here, denied the lad so soon.
    A flask of water dangles to a nail,
And here a can of powder; candles there,
    A pair of scissors, and a bunch of quills.
Their dinners lie beside them, and beyond
Are drills and hammers and long iron bars.
Ere they begin to labour, child and sire
Kneel down among the rocks, and that dark cave
    Is visited by angels, whose bright wings
Float through the darkness to the voice of prayer.
    Aloud the father intercedes with Heaven
    For blessings on the labour of their hands,
    And blessings on his darling ones at home,
That He would spare them, if it were His will,
    To meet at eve around the supper board.
    But if they fell and died among the rocks,
He pray'd that they might dwell in heaven, and sit
    Down at the marriage-supper of the Lamb.
    And then he wrestled for his comrade-boy;
    And in his earnestness he seem'd to grasp
    The arm of the Most High, and so prevail'd
That heaven kiss'd earth and dropp'd into the mine.
Could you have peer'd into that youngling's face,
    Hidden in both his hands, you would have seen
Great shining tear-drops roll down on the stones.
    That boy grew up to bear the cross of Christ.

THE MINE
Part 2

Years stole away; the rich mine richer grew;
Another lode was added richer still:
It strangely shot out in the engine-shaft,
And so he hail'd it as a friend with gems,
Who came to pour the treasures in his lap.
It was a vein of copper bright as brass,
Which soon became the theme at every hearth.
Copper has colours different in the ores,
As various as the rainbow, – black and blue
And green and red and yellow as a flower;
Gold-coloured here, there dimly visible,
Though rich the same in measure and in meed.
'tis found alike where glittering granite gloams,
Where killas darkens, and where gossans shroud,
And oft where wise ones write it cannot be, –
Thus wisely scatter'd by the Hand Divine.
Tin is more secret far, with duller eye
Oft hiding in the river's shingly bed,
Or the flint's bosom, near the central fires,
In chambers wide, or veins like silken lace;
So that the labourer, stumbling on a start,
Wipes his hot brow, and cries, "Lo, here is tin."

Then on the miner dawn'd a brighter day,
A day to be remember'd, when the fuse
Was first invented by ingenious minds, –
A miracle for safety and for price.
How many lives has it been blest to save
And families from mourning ! Ages hence
Our wise posterity will hail its birth,
A bright star in the dim sky of the past,
And clothe the inventors' honour'd busts with fame.

The slime of earth is only on the skin;
That of the serpent stains into the soul.
The Cornish miner, pale and sulphur-streak'd,
Basks in the brightness of the eternal Sun,
And muses through the halls of intellect
As largely as the man of wealth and power,
And walks as blest with calm-eyed Piety.
Behold him in his honeysuckled cot,

Kissing his children in the day's young prime,
Even while they lie sweet-smiling in their dreams;
Then hasting forth with prayer upon his lips
To tug with Danger in his darksome den
Beneath the hills' foundations. Noon arrives,
And in a level far below the light,
With flint on either hand, a band of men,
From different chambers of the mighty cave,
Frieze on their loins and slime upon their limbs,
Sing, pray, and praise the Lord. and fruit Divine
Is gather'd by them from the banks of bliss.

Old Timmy was the driver of the mules,
And he kept sixty shaggy skinny things,
Fed upon grass and very little grain;
And with his mules he visited the mine,
A tramping troop, to carry off the ores
In little bags upon their bony backs,
Two upon each, up hill and down deep dale,
To the sea-port where it was shipp'd away
Across the waves, and fused to metal slabs.
And years pass'd by, and still he drove his mules
Through cloud and sunshine, storm and pleasing calm,
Summer and winter, smoking as he went,
Or whistling tunes and cracking his short whip,
Telling strange tales to singing birds and flowers,
Familiar with each hedge, and crooked turn,
And ragged rut from long lane's end to end,
Till he grew grey as the grey herd he drove:
Then, as the ores increased, the farmers came,
With waggons wide and woeful, and lean steeds,
Which panted o'er the highways rough and rude,
With perspiration dropping off like rain, –
A sight to sadden every sorrowing heart.
But one spring morn, awaking from his dreams,
He heard the steam-horse rushing o'er the rails,
Bearing more ores behind it than his troop
Could carry in a fortnight. So he turn'd
His old friends on the common, where they fail'd,
And failing fail'd, till they could fail no more,
And Winter slew them with his sword of frost.
He could not weep, for all his tears were gone;
And in his reedy lodge a heavy sigh

Let out his ghost into the land unseen.
His grave is by the chancel of the church;
And on it many years a grave-board stood;
But time has blotted out the epitaph,
And left him sleeping in a nameless shroud.

A travelling youth hastes down the village lane
All fever'd with excitement. By the well
He meets a matron with her jar and jug;
And as she dips them in the crystal fount,
He asks her, pointing with his hazel staff,
"Who lives across the coppice in yon house
They say was haunted many years ago?
Though for my part I can't believe a ghost
Would quit the bowers of angels for this place,
To dwell with rats and cobwebs. Fie on it!
I've heard my father say how oft strange lights
Would flare along the damp rooms windowless,
And solemn dirges at still midnight rose,
And songs were heard when nought but winds were there:
And so the people said the manor-house
Was haunted with the strangest, wildest things.
Old women's fancies! why, I've walked o'er graves,
And fields of dead, and mounds of rotting bones,
When stars were blinking in the deeps of heaven;
And I have often pray'd to see a ghost,
If ghosts are palpable to mortal ken –:
But not a phantom raised his shadowy arm.
When last I saw this dwelling, years ago,
't was weeping in its ruins: now it looks
The abode of plenty, where red faces meet.
Pray, can you tell me who the owner is?"
And when she told him that its present lord
Was once the tinner living on the moor,
Who ventured till the mice forsook his shelf
And leanness seized upon him, he exclaim'd,
"O change of changes! 't is my father's home."

Full soon he cross'd the greenwood, praising much
The grand old trees that seem'd to welcome him
To linger in their cloisters. Then he stood
Within the ivy archway, lost in thought.
And now his hands are playing with the vine

About the porch; and now he knocks the door,
And soon is weeping in his mother's arms.
Then father comes, but how unlike the man
He left half-starved within his frigid hut,
Still struggling, striving, hoping against hope!
A portly person now with manly air,
And much that's pleasant peering from his eye.
Then tales were told and loving questions ask'd,
And lengthy queries answer'd, till the moon
Slid into midnight with her suite of stars,
And prayer uprose among the listening trees.
Then he lay down to dream of other days,
And one bright vision flitted though his brain.

Next morn his father took him on a hill
Within his own estate, where cattle grazed
And finest sheep were feeding. Far below,
Upon the very spot the dragon roll'd
Where the bold honest tinner lost and won,
A mine spread out its vast machinery.
Here engines, with their huts and smoky stacks,
Cranks, wheels, and rods, boilers and hissing steam,
Press'd up the water from the depths below.
Here fire-whims ran till almost out of breath,
And chains cried sharply, strain'd with fiery force.
Here blacksmiths hammer'd by the sooty forge,
And there a crusher crash'd the copper ore.
Here girls were cobbing under roofs of straw,
And there were giggers at the oaken hutch.
Here a man-engine glided up and down,
A blessing and a boon to mining men:
And near the spot where, many years before,
Turn'd round and round the rude old water-wheel,
A huge fire-stamps was working evermore,
And slimy boys were swarming at the trunks.
The noisy lander by the trap-door bawl'd
With pincers in his hand; and troops of maids
With heavy hammers brake the mineral stones.
The cart-man cried, and shook his broken whip;
And on the steps of the account-house stood
The active agent, with his eye on all.

Below were caverns grim with greedy gloom,
And levels drunk with darkness; chambers huge
Where Fear sat silent, and the mineral-sprite
    For ever chanted his bewitching song;
Shafts deep and dreadful, looking darkest things
And seeming almost running down to doom;
Rock under foot, rock standing on each side;
    Rock cold and gloomy, frowning overhead;
    Before, behind, at every angle, rock.
Here blazed a vein of precious copper ore,
Where lean men labour'd with a zeal for fame,
With face and hands and vesture black as night,
    And down their sides the perspiration ran
    In steaming eddies, sickening to behold.
But they complain'd not, digging day and night,
And morn and eve, with lays upon their lips.
Here yawn'd a tin-cell like a cliff of crags,
And Danger lurk'd among the groaning rocks,
And ofttimes moan'd in darkness. All the air
Was black with sulphur, burning up the blood.
A nameless mystery seem'd to fill the void,
And wings all pitchy flapp'd among the flints,
And eyes that saw not sparkled mid the spars.
Yet here men work'd, on stages hung in ropes,
With drills and hammers blasting the rude earth,
Which fell with such a crash that he who heard
Cried, "Jesu, save the miner!" Here were ends
Cut through hard marble by the miners' skill,
And winzes, stopes, and rises: pitches here,
Where work'd the heroic, princely tributer,
This month for nothing, next for fifty pounds.
Here lodes ran wide, and there so very small
That scarce a pick-point could be press'd between;
Here making walls as smooth as polish'd steel,
    And there as craggy as a rended hill:
    And out of sparry vagues the water oozed.
Staining the rock with mineral, so that oft
    It led the labourer to a house of gems.
Across the mine a hollow cross-course ran
From north to south, an omen of much good;
And tin lay heap'd on stulls and level-plots;
And in each nook a tallow taper flared,

84

Where pale men wasted with exhaustion huge.
Here holes exploded, and there mallets rang,
And rocks fell crashing, lifting the stiff hair
From time-worn brows, and noisy buckets roar'd
In echoing shafts; and through this gulf of gloom
A hollow murmur rush'd for evermore.

And then the father and his wondering boy
Cross'd the rude moors, conversing as they went,
When the youth learnt his father sold the mine
For thousands upon thousands, keeping still
Large shares of profit for himself and son.
And as they linger'd by a broken stile,
Watching a flock of rooks wheel o'er the wood,
And breathing odours from the banks of flowers,
A group of mining men came down the lane,
With footsteps fleet, and very sad of face,
Bearing a burden on some unplaned boards
Nail'd carelessly together. 't was a youth
Who left his mother on the lonely wild
At dead of night, to dig within the mine.
He was her only son; the rest were drown'd,
And so this boy became her sole support.
And rumour ran he courted a fair maid,
Whose fame was like a rose-bud, and next moon
They would be married in the village church.
But Providence had order'd otherwise;
For while he labour'd, tamping up a hole
In a hard cross-cut, ninety fathoms down,
It crash'd around him, killing him outright;
And so his mangled form, lash'd to a spar,
Was drawn up through the shaft, and borne along
By his sad comrades to his mother's hut;
And fleetly pass'd they over hill and dale,
Till lost among the rising mists of morn.

There was a miner living by a rock
They call'd "The Giant's Marble:" with him dwelt
His wife and six young children, and he strove
By dint of labour with his head and hands,
Early and late, above ground and below,
Both in his little farm and in his pitch,
With manly courage wondrous and sublime, –

More of the hero than the man of spears, –
To feed the flock the Shepherd of the world
Placed in his fold upon the brambled plain.
But months pass'd by, and he no mineral found
Within the rock he blasted: pay-days came,
But not for him; and on his famish'd cheek
Despair had almost stamp'd his frightful name.
Late one long eve the weary tributer
Was digging in the darkness, when he found
A prill of copper larger than his fist,
Which led the labourer to a course of ore;
And ere three weeks had pass'd, the worthy man
Had gain'd enough to cheer his drooping wife,
To pay his debts, and buy his pretty farm.
A cottage girl is wandering by a brook,
Gathering wild flowers, and singing, "From the isles
My love is coming with his heart for me.
His letters have been sweet with tenderest lore,
And musical with gladness. Since he left,
His sire one morn awoke in rifled rags;
And ere the sun went down behind the waves,
He was a rich man, courted and caress'd.
And will success estrange my only love,
And lure him to some less devoted maid?
Away with such a thought! it cannot be;
And so I'll pluck these flowers to bind his brow,
And kiss them as they smile baptized with dews.
He loves the primrose: thus, ye cherubs, come,
And let me pull you for an offering sweet."
And as she drew them from their homes of moss,
Pressing them gently in her little hand,
A fair young man came tripping down the banks,
With summer sunshine glowing in his face.
It was her Henry, and full soon their tears
And sighs and kisses mingle as they flow.

"Why do the bells ring out such merry chimes?"
An aged dame ask'd, pausing on the road
To meet her daughter from the market town
With basket huge and heavy. "All this morn
A sea of echoes has been rolling round,

So that the rooks have scarcely had a note
To offer to the sunshine; peal on peal
Has travell'd through the valleys, and the hills
Have almost thrust their ragged caps aside.
I've seen the horses prick their pointed ears,
And pause amid the clover; and the dogs
Have bark'd and danced, not knowing what they did.
Boys clap their hands and maidens sing for glee,
And matrons, arms a-kimbo o'er the fence
Converse and smile, and kiss their wondering bairns.
Why, every tree now shining in the sun
Seems wagging with a bell upon each branch.
I never heard such stunning peals before;
No, not when our good squire and lady fair
In bridal robes walk'd to the dear old church.
Do tell me, daughter, why the bells ring so."

"It is a marriage, mother. The rich man
Who lives in yon high house across the gorge,
Environ'd with a wood of English oak,
Who drew his riches from a mining pit
When almost dead with fasting, this still morn
Has seen his son united to a girl
As beautiful as summer, whom he loved
When Want stood shivering in his father's home
With Famine on the doorstep. Far away
The young man laboured, prosper'd, and return'd
To find his father rich in friends and fame,
Himself a partner in his hard-earn'd gains.
But richer to his eye the cottage girl,
Who sang among the green fields like a bird,
Than heaps of diamonds piled up to the moon,
Or farms, or friends, or any other thing:
For he was true, and love to him was heaven.
So they are married, mother, and the bells
Ring that the grand old steeple seems to nod.
And let them peal still louder, louder still:
A pair more worthy never were made one,
Since Adam Eve took from the hands of God."

See'st thou that mansion on the woody slope,
Where trees stoop down and kiss the river-waves,
Or whisper on its marge; and graceful sails

Glide up and down, and sea-birds float and dive?
Along the shrubbery walk a lady comes
Leading her children by the evergreens, –
Two boys, with brows like bards and eyes like space;
And one bright girl, with April on her cheeks.
Grey deer are leaping round them, snowy swans
Steer over silent lakes, and cooing doves
Drop from tall trees to drink at glassy falls,
Whilst in the noble dwelling Wealth sits down
Dangling his shining keys with wagging sides.
This hall is Henry's, his that lady fair,
And his those children beautiful as morn.
Such has old Cornwall lifted from her mines,
The God of Providence directing them,
And placed among the worshipp'd of the world.
And thousands yet to come will bless the hour
That drew them forth to drain her mineral-veins.

GLOSSARY OF MINING TERMS

Adit – An opening beneath the surface of the earth, to carry off the water from the mine.

Cobbing – Breaking the stones with an iron hammer, to separate the mineral from the refuse.

Course of ore – A wide vein or lode.

Cross-course – A hollow vein intersecting the lodes.

Cross-cut – A level driven to intersect .the lode.

Crusher – A sort of iron mill used to crush the ore.

Dowzing-rod – A white thorn used by the ancient miners to ascertain the position of uncut lodes.

Dragon – A fiery meteor, said to be indicative of the earth's riches.

Drill – A bar of steel used for boring the rock.

End – A local name for level, the extremity of the subterranean passage.

Fire-stamps – A steam-engine used to stamp the rough ores.

Fire-whim – A small steam-engine used to draw up the broken earth.

Fuse – A flexible material, similar to common yarn, bound with twine, and filled with gunpowder; used in blasting.

Gigger – One who sifts the ores through a small sieve into a hutch or large box of water.

Gossan – Consists principally of per-oxide of iron, mixed with earthy matters, quartz,etc.

Killas – A dark-coloured stratum of rock, composed of clay, slate, etc

Lander – The man who empties the bucket when it reaches the mouth of the pit.

Level – An excavation along the mine.

Level-plot – A floor of wood where the miner fills the bucket.

Lode – A mineral deposit, generally running from east to west.

Man-engine – A machine to let the miners up and down the shaft.

Pitches – Cells of copper or any other mineral, where the labourer has a certain tribute.

Prill – A lump of solid mineral or metal.

Rises – Chambers raised from beneath.

Smelting-house – A place where raw ores are converted by fire into metal.

Start or sturt – Among miners an extra month's wages; chiefly, the good fortune of tributers.

Stopes – The upper or lower parts of levels broken up by miners.

Stulls – Large beams of wood across the lode, on which rough boards are nailed.

Tinner – One who works on tin.

Tributer – One who works for a certain part of the profits of the ores he may raise.

Trunks – Hutches let into the ground.

Windlass – A simple roller of wood with an iron handle, around which is wound a rope or chain, which is let up and down the pit.

Winze – A sink from one level to another.

Unpublished Poems
From the John Harris Autobiography (1882)

The Miller and His Nag

What a snug little place was the miller's abode,
In a sycamore dell by the side of the road!
And his bright little boy from his cottage would steal,
And clap his small hands at the sound of the wheel.

The miller would hug him and kiss him once more,
Then point him to pony so sleek at the door,
Who never had lash-cord or leather-thong yet,
Since granny had called him the miller boy's pet.

He came at their call, he would feed from their hand,
And by the low stepping-block quietly stand,
Or carefully clamber the moorland ascent,
As the miller rode town-wards to settle his rent.

"I never beat pony," the miller would say,
"No matter how lengthened, how rugged the way;
A chirp or a whistle sufficeth for him,
Who trots on all day till the twilight is dim."

"A pat on his neck has more power than the lash,
And a kind word is stronger than the oak-bough or ash."
So sing with the miller, who strikes not a blow,
"No whip for my pony wherever we go."

The Daisy Meadow

Dear image of the dainty spring!
My heart is cheered by thee;
One scene which thou wert sure to bring
Is evermore with me –
A meadow of my father's farm,
Where I would roam for hours,
With my dear harp upon my arm,
All white with daisy flowers.

't was called by us the Under Field,
And there the lambkins played,
When violet-fairies donned their shield
In many a mossy glade.
But nought to me was half so dear,
Which loving Nature dowers,
As this small meadow by the mere
All white with daisy flowers.

The hum of insects met my ear,
The gorse in gold was dressed,
And underneath the hawthorn near
The robin built it's nest;
The lark it's sweetest song did yield,
Which fell in liquid showers;
O, nought was like the Under Field
All white with daisy flowers.

In ranks behind, in ranks before,
They wooed the summer air,
A countless host, a starry floor,
They kissed each other there.
And even now my heart is healed,
Though sorrows come in showers,
When thinking of the Under Field
All white with daisy flowers.

It comes in evening's twilight dreams,
When song is on the floods,
And music in unnumbered streams
Floats through the leafy woods.
With charms to deaden worldly care,
And melt the cloud which lowers,
The Under Field, which hides the hare
All white with daisy flowers.

Nor will it fade from memory's eye,
From memory's treasured store,
Till darkness shadow earth and sky,
And life itself is o'er
A bliss by hidden hands unsealed,
To cheer my latest hours,
Is that hill-sloping Under Field
All white with daisy flowers.

My Early Home

When starting tears are in mine eye,
And rises oft the bursting sigh,
When careless words oppress my soul,
And noisy tongues of torture roll,
My thoughts unfettered, fly at will
To my dear cottage on the hill.

When I am weary with life's march,
Beneath some pride-erected arch,
Where pipers play, whose numbers roar,
Like potsherds grating on the shore,
The lark is with me sweetly-shrill
Above the heather of my hill.

When I am wandering sadly on,
My lyre unstrung, its music gone,
Where sounds of anguish fill my ears,
And sorrow's face is stained with tears,
The rustling ferns, the rippling rill,
Are with me on my dear old hill.

And when, like Jonah, low I lie,
And feel t'wer better far to die,
My earth-gourds gone, my props decayed,
And dry wells open in the glade,
A solace for my sorrows still
Is my dear boulder-covered hill.

When ranked with those who scarcely know
Why oceans ebb, or currents flow,
To whom the printer's page is less,
Than flounces on my lady's dress,
With gushing drops my eyes will fill
For years of music on the hill.

And ask you why I ever turn
To these lone heights so still and stern?
A mother there, a father good,
And brothers mid the thyme-banks stood.
Where Nature gave her child his quill,
And God is on my native hill.

The Drunken Father

A dirty alehouse stands
Upon the country green,
And by the midnight fire
A ragged man is seen,
O, haggard is his cheek,
And rolls his vacant eye!
And underneath his rimless hat
Long knotted tresses lie.

A lonely little girl
Comes almost out of breath,
And her sweet voice is heard
Within this den of death.
"O, father, haste with me,
Mother lies on the straw!
She says she's dying, and her breath,
How hard it seems to draw!"

"Go home, you dirty thing,
And don't disturb me here;
But leave me at my fiery sport,
My jolly boys, and beer.
So ho, let's merry be,
And smother shaking care,
Till Morning dances on the sea,
With sunbeams in her hair."

Again, that weeping child
Came pleading to her sire;
Again, her father thrust her off,
With a dark drunkard's ire.
And when her little feet
Re-echoed in their shed,
Her loving mother on the straw
Was lying pale and dead!

The Bright Path

One track is like a track of gold,
My boyhood's feet have trod,
'tis with me up and down the earth,
Wherever I may plod,
In budding spring, in summer time
And when the winds are cool –
The narrow path through Rickard's Moor
That led to Forest school.

The moss cups on the violet banks,
The brooklet glancing clear,
Were whispering like the voice of love
When Primrose-tufts appear.
O, I was taught by birds that fly,
And fishes in the pool
Beside the path through Rickard's Moor
That led to Forest School.

Down hill we ran with nimble feet
Among the furze and heath,
Where, mid the masses of bog-peat,
The rushes shone beneath.

I left my mother at her task,
My marbles by the stool,
To tread the path through Rickard's Moor
That led to Forest school.

And now I seem to hear again
The tinkle of the stream,
The lark's song o'er the sunny bowers
Where fern-hid fairies dream;
To tread once more the springy turf,
Where brooklets murmur cool,
Along the path through Rickard's Moor
That led to Forest school.

What is it in the human heart
That chance and change outlives,
Unconquered by the crush of years?
The love which nature gives.
Yet more and more this narrow track
Gleams by the rushy pool
Along the path through Rickard's Moor
That led to Forest school.

Spring

From the doorway of the south,
Whence the breeze is stealing,
Comes young spring, with gentle voice,
O'er the meadows pealing.
Here a darling crocus peeps,
There a primrose yellow,
And the violet by the brook
Noddeth to its fellow.

Larks are scattering songs around,
Early trees are sprouting,
Ploughman whistles o'er the ground,
All the winds are shouting.
Valleys tell the valleys much
Of the days a-coming,
And the rivers roll their joy
Where the woods are humming.

Mosses fill their cups with wine
For the coming fairies,
And the vernal rain-drops shine
Where the landscape varies.
Life is stirring in the sap
Of the Withered larches,
And the rose half-shows its bud
In the forest arches.

Robin calls his mate to build,
By the hawthorn bushes,
While the dingle rings its joy,
Redolent with thrushes.
God is speaking in the earth
Of our daily duty,
Soon will come the happy May
Rich in bud and beauty.

My Treasures

I still have you, my darlings,
When wayside waters flow,
And larks sing o'er the meadows
On cloudlets white as snow;
I still have you – the daisy,
The lily and the rose,
Which man can not deny me,
And Providence bestows.

Ye talk to me in hedges,
Ye whisper on the hills,
Unseal your urns in dingles
Where turn the watermills,
As foamy rivers tumble
Among the towering trees,
And airs which poets gather
Are floating on the breeze.

Ye cannot snatch the flowerets
Up from my daily track,
Though fickle fortune's vintage
Ye coldly let me lack.

O, one dear sun-born blossom,
Within the sheltered glen,
Where Meditation museth,
Is worth a thousand men.

I still have you, dear wildings,
On pastures, peak, and plain,
Where winds weave endless story,
So I will not complain;
No! though I eat my morsel
Unbuttered by the log,
And scarcely have a fragment
To feed my hungry dog.

I still have you, my darlings;
My bank and spreading beech,
With more of heavenly wisdom
Than all the pulpits teach:
For God's own voice is speaking
Where'er your bright eyes be,
"O, bending child of sorrow,
Look up! And trust in me."

The Faces at the Pane

Where e'er I go, What e'er I do,
A vision meets mine eye
From the far valleys of the past,
Flecked with the summer sky.
It comes in days of quiet trust,
It comes in wind and rain,
It comes when harvest crowns the earth –
The faces at the pane.

When toiling in the darksome mine,
As tired as tired can be,
How has the glad thought cheered my soul, –
My children watch for me!
And so I oped the garden gate,
Which led into the lane,
How danced my heart to see once more
The faces at the pane!

Two little girls, with gleaming eyes,
With soft and shining hair,
And sweetest prattle on their lips,
Were watching for me there.
One in the grave is sleeping now,
And one has crossed the main;
Yet still I see, Where e'er I be,
The faces at the pane.

And when I brought some hedgerow fruit,
Or darling hedgerow flowers,
Which they were early taught to love,
Their kisses came in showers.
O, precious were those distant days,
Which may not come again,
Made brighter, fairer, fresher for
The faces at the pane.

Old age has bound me in its bands,
And o'er the solemn sea
I seem to hear mysterious sounds
From unknown lake and lea.
But through the cares that lie behind,
Along the murky plain,
I see, as if but yesterday,
The faces at the pane.

Few retrospects have greater joy,
Now life is waning fast,
And fewer visions sun my soul
Like this from out the past.
And thank I Him who giveth much
Our gratitude to gain,
Nor least among His greater gifts
The faces at the pane.

The Cornish Huer *

The Huer is out on the hills away,
And his eyes are fixed on the distant bay.
There are no signs of fish in the offing now,
And he waits with his arm on a pine-tree's bough,
Half-rent when the northern winds were up,
And the sea foam whitened the Giant's cup.

They come, they come, that longed-for shoal,
And his voice goes forth in a welcome roll
Over rock and reef, over lake and land,
Where huts are hidden in creeks of sand;
And the hardy fishers are at their oars,
And their glad wives watch them from their doors.

Heave ho! Heave ho! The nets are cast,
The shining fish are enclosed at last.
The boats are filled – they row to shore,
Hurrah! Hurrah! They return once more,
A harvest to reap for "one and all."
Hurrah for the Huer who gives the call!

* *The Cornish Huer is one who is stationed on the hills, near the cliffs, in the pilchard season, to give the word of warning on the approach of a shoal of fish, when the boats at once put out to secure them.*

Summer Rain

How gently it falls from the quiet sky,
On the lonely mead and the mountain high!
No voice of wind, no rush of gale,
No echo of storm in the leafy vale,
But soft as a fairy tapping the pane
When the moon is full, is the summer rain.

The thirsty flowers by the moorland streams,
And the hedgerow bends where the ivy gleams
Drink in the drops, as they gently fall
Pat, pat on the leaves, with a good for all;
And they whisper it over, and over again,
"Thanks, thanks for the freshening summer rain."

The fox-glove longed for the drops to come,
And the daisy pined in its lowly home,
The wild rose drooped on the dusty spray,
And the woodbine wept by the lone highway,
Till they quickly felt revived again
In the silent, softening summer rain.

How gently it comes! And who can tell
Its blest results on field and fell,
On garden bower, and corn-mead green,
And where the fruit mid the leaves is seen:
Or the grasses bend on the thirsty plain
In the silent, softening summer rain!

So God's free grace in silence falls,
When the waiting one in spirit calls,
And the quiet worker is often blest
By him who soothes the seas to rest,
And the flowers appear on the gladdened plain,
In the silent, softening Spirit's rain.

The Strong Smith by the Sea

In the peaceful days to be
Worked a strong smith by the sea,
Chanting thus, with bosom bare,
"The sword I change to the shining share."

Heaps of spears in his smithy lay,
Blades gore-dyed in the fearful fray,
And the sparks rose high on the morning air
As the sword was changed to the shining share.

And loud the monster bellows roared,
Reddening many an ancient sword.
"This is the way" sang the strong smith there,
"To change the spear to the shining share."

The great wind came from the northern moor,
And shook the walls from roof to floor;
But that steady smith, in the forge's glare,
Still changed the sword to the shining share.

And ever that strong man laboured he,
Summer and winter beside the sea,
With heavy hammer and bosom bare,
Till the swords were changed to the shining share.

Apparently first published by John Harris in his 'The Cruise of the Cutter and other Poems (London, Partridge & Co., 1872,) pp 5-6, then later reproduced in his larger 'Wayside Pictures, Hymns and Poems' (London, Hamilton, Adams & Co., 1874, p.234 Five four-line verses.

When First I Saw the Sea

A picture bright with trees and flowers,
Green mead's with daisies drest,
And little hills when morning breaks
With sunlight on their crest;
Lakes shining where the willows bend;
As homewards hums the bee,
Is that blest hour, so long ago,
When first I saw the sea.

My loving father took me there,
One morn in early spring,
When o'er the carns and mountain meads
The larks did soar and sing.
How I enjoyed the winding lanes,
The stream, the floweret's bell,
The landscape stretching far away,
No tongue on earth can tell.

The sea in all its grandeur lay
Beyond my father's door,
Though we could see it from the hill
Ten Cornish miles or more.
And nine long years have passed away,
Within our home inland,
Before my feet had borne me there,
Or trod its shining sand.

And when the huge rocks rose to view,
As the great cliff came near
And ocean's everlasting voice
Broke on my ravished ear,
The mystery of that solemn scene,
In sunlight robes arrayed,
Where grandeur sang its loftiest hymn,
Can never be portrayed.

And when at eve the chimney-nook
Beheld me with my pen,
The sound, the sight, the rock, the roar,
The spell, were with me then.
And sitting at my mother's side,
Who turned her griefs to gold,
By loving intercourse with Him,
O what a tale I told!

No vision has a brighter tint,
With rainbow hues o'ercast,
Arising with a rush of joy
Out of the solemn past,
Than this which now I simply sing,
As old Time hurries he, –
The sunny, silent, April morn,
When first I saw the sea.

This came from a posthumous work, on the cover of which is the title 'Last Lays' /John Harris but actually the title-page has: 'Nan Neva' a Cornish Story, with Domestic Poems by John Harris (Falmouth, The Author's Sons, Killigrew Terrace-Penryn, John Gill & Son – Exeter, F. Clapp, Roseneath, St Jame's road, 1884).The Preface note (p.iv) is by the sons and states that this is from a M S. completed 'shortly before his decease – January 7th, 1884'.

When First I Saw The Sea is dated 'February 21st, 1883', pp.68 – 69. We can identify this as referring to the North Cliffs between Hells Mouth and Portreath, because another poem in the same book – pp.108-109 – is called Sprat-in-Cove,dated; 'June 9th. 1883', and refers to this same first visit. The Cove in question is usually called 'Spratting Cove' and is on the North Cliffs near Carvannel and Tehidy Woods.

Sprat-in-Cove

The Ivy round my native rocks
Was green as green can be,
When I went off to Sprat-in-Cove,
Where rolls the northern sea.
A noisy fair was held in town,
Where painted showmen bawled;
But I went off to Sprat-in-Cove,
Because the Muses called.

The earth was green, the skies were blue,
The lark was overhead,
As I went off to Sprat-in-Cove,
By nature's organ led.
The clown might prance,
the showmen dance,
The mountebanks might roar,
But I was off to Sprat-in-Cove,
To tread its sandy shore.

The billows tumbled at my feet
With lays from Isles of green,
And on their foam-crests wondrous shapes
At every roll was seen.

And as the murmur filled my soul,
I felt delighted there.
That I came off to Sprat-in-Cove
While Robby went to fair.

The shepherd taught me with his sheep,
The white gulls floating round,
The mermaid sporting in her cave,
With belts of seaweed bound.
The fair! I never thought of it,
Old ocean's grots among,
As I mused down in Sprat-in-Cove,
And bathed myself in song.

The pleasure which this visit gave
Is with me till this day,
As voices o'er the wilderness
Are calling me away.
And thank I Him whose word of truth
Gives eyesight to the blind,
That I went off to Sprat-in-Cove,
And left the crowd behind.

Uncle Will and the Extinguished Candle

UNCLE Will and the writer of this sketch were working together underground, digging in a singularly narrow place after copper ore. It was in a very unfrequented part of the mine, where the sound of another miner's hammer was not heard on the rock. Uncle Will was an old man, and I let him sit upon a board a very little way behind the working, charging him to take care and keep his light burning, while I used the pick and iron wedges in cutting through the lode. Nearly half an hour, perhaps, had thus passed, and not a word had been spoken between us, when, by some mischance, I happened to strike the candle which gave us light in the working, and which was stuck to a fragment of the rock with soft clay, called Saint Ann's, with the point of the pick, knocking it among the rubbish, so that it was extinguished immediately.

Looking back at Uncle Will I was perfectly astounded to find that his candle, too, was gone out, with the exception of a spark of fire in the wick, at which the old man was blowing with all his might, endeavouring in vain to enkindle it. A puff or two more, and we were in utter darkness. I questioned my unwatchful comrade about it, and his reply was, "Oh, dear! I caught a nod, and awoke just in time to see my candle falling."

And now what could we do? To cry for help would be utterly useless; as well might the wrecked mariner, floating on a board, call to the moon. To sound the rock and give the understood signal with miners, would also be fruitless, as we were too isolated for anything of that sort. Nor had we any means to strike a light, for this occurred before Lucifer matches had been invented. If we remained there, it might be many days before any help reached us, and in that time we should suffer much from hunger and thirst, and perhaps die of starvation. Seeing our position thus critically extreme, I addressed Uncle Will, saying there was no alternative for us but to endeavour to grope our way through the great darkness to the top of the mine.

It was a serious undertaking, but the only way at all likely to prove effectual. Better run this risk than sit there to die of cold and hunger in the sickly, sulphurous cell. Should we try? And Uncle Will answered, "Yes."

Taking a pick in my hand to feel the way, I went before, and Uncle Will followed after. How slowly we advanced! Sometimes we had to ascend the face of the rock, where little notches were cut for our feet, the omission of one of which would be swift destruction. Sometimes we had a ladder to climb, and land upon the narrowest platform, full of holes, where a slip of the foot would be our ruin. Sometimes we had low workings to crawl through, where we could not stand upright, and flinty rocks to scramble over with teeth as sharp as swords. Then we had long levels to pass through, in which were deep sinks, with only a single narrow plank across them, which warped and bent as we came upon it, crawling over on our hands and knees.

I often had to cheer Uncle Will with words of encouragement, bidding him to keep directly behind me, while we felt our way inch by inch, and foot by foot, with the pick handle. Now we had a set of ladders to mount, shifting this way and that way as we reached the top of one to gain the foot of the other, the ascent being no wider than an ordinary well. Slowly, silently and solemnly we went; and in the pauses of our steps we could hear the beating of our heart against our side. A single slip of the foot, and we should be lost in some grim excavation where we might lie undiscovered until the sea gave up her dead, and the earth put on her flaming funeral shroud.

Whenever we could, we felt the rock at our side, or under our feet; and with our previous acquaintance with the way, having been over it so often before, we knew within a few yards where we were. But now we had to pass by a shaft, where the footway was not more than three feet wide, which yawned under us some two hundred fathoms deep. There was no chain, or rope, or railing around it, or security of any kind. It was useless to strain our eyes to try to catch a gleam of light; We might as well have kept them closed, for the great gloom was as perfect as that in the house of the dead.

This shaft was the most dangerous part of the way; and I cannot tell the reader how slowly we passed it. Sometimes a loose stone, disturbed by our movements, would roll into the void, and go sounding down the dreadful depths, until we could hear it no longer. Thus we stole onward, with the thought of home wife and children in our minds. Could we cross this cruel gulf, hope would revive, for then the ladders would almost be in direct perpendicular line to the top. At last we got over, and Uncle Will and his guide were again ascending. We felt now comparatively safe.

This was the regularly-used way up and down the mine, and we might, perhaps, soon meet someone with a light; and if not, we felt almost certain of reaching the top. Up we go, up, up; ladder after ladder, ladder after ladder, each round bringing us nearer to liberty and home. By and bye, when looking upward, we saw a speck of light like a distant star in the firmament, and as we ascended higher, it became larger, and larger, until its cheering rays shot down the ladder steps, gladdening our hearts more than the sweetest music.

Grasping the last ladder, we felt the tears of thankfulness stealing into our eyes; and reaching the topmost round, and stepping into the dazzling light, we had to wipe them away with the sleeve of our flannel dress. We were saved by the guiding hand of our Father out of the darksome dungeon into the blessed air and glorious sunshine! Yes, by untiring, persevering effort, we had climbed into the light.

And so shall it be with him who mourns in secret and trustfully lays his troubles before his maker. Art though sitting in darkness, poor weary one? And is thy candle extinguished in the conflict like those of the two miners in the depths of the earth?

To remain thus, without an effort on thy part is eternal ruin. Arise and climb towards him who is the Light of the world, and every step shall bring thee nearer to the region of purest joy, where the Sun of Righteousness rains His splendour on the lovely land. Is thy daily labour much, and thy bread little, and do thy hungry children often look towards the empty cupboard and ask for food in vain?

Tell it to Him who is the Guider of His people. Fling away thy garment, and kneel before the Son of David, and in his own time deliverance shall come; the beauty of heaven shall beam upon thy path, and the shadows of sorrow flee away. Step by step, and the desert is passed; the gloomy ravine is left behind; the rugged ridge is surmounted, and the Canaan of repose is reached, which hath no need of the sun neither of the moon to shine in it; for the Glory of God doth lighten it, and the Lamb is the Light thereof.

Old Granny Bent

A widow was Granny much wasted with care,
And bright lines of silver had mixed with her hair:
Her thin cheeks were worn with the sorrows of years;
Deep channels were there, as if washed out with tears,
She stooped a bit forward, wherever she went,
And the villagers knew her as old Granny Bent.

She lived in a little house by the moor stream,
And her window was gilt with the morning's first beam.
The Ivy had climbed all the way to the thatch,
And the woodbine was whispering over the latch,
Where the rose and the myrtle were lovingly blent
On the walls of the dwelling of old Granny Bent.

There neatness and cleaness with order combined,
And her pewter was bright as the spade of a hind;
The cat by the cricket coiled up in its place,
Where the sands of the hour-glass were running their race;
And the musk in the window out-wafted its scent
To comfort the croonings of old Granny Bent.

The parish allowed her the dole of its poor,
Yet the beggar unaided ne'er passed from her door:
And 'twas sweet, when the elder came out by the gate,
As in the low porch-way she silently sate,
Gazing down the wide moor on the twilight's descent,
To hear the bright needles of old Granny Bent.

She read but one book in the heat and the cold:
Its pages were tear-marked, its covers were old,
And over the leaves above and below
Some joy lines were visible, made long ago.
Its precepts she pondered wherever she went;
The Bible was precious to old Granny Bent.

When the Sabbeth bells sounded along the green leas,
She went to her meeting-house under the trees;
And here I have seen her with trust in her eye,
When waiting in silence for Him to pass by;
Imploring in breathings the Spirit's descent,
Who came in His beauty to old Granny Bent.

One morning I missed her. The warning had come,
And the Angel of mercy had summoned her home.
Below we were seeking the aid of His rod;
On high she was hymning the praises of God.
And this was my thought on the solemn event;
What a change up in glory for old Granny Bent!

Old Frankey

Old Frankey sat in his elbow chair;
His visage was pale and marked with care,
His wife and he had both grown old,
And their son had left them in search of gold.

Old Frankey's wife, with a look of dread,
Told how the cupboard contained no bread;
And "What shall we do?" with a sigh began;
"O, trust in God !" said the dear old man.

Then he climbed the stairs with his locks so grey.
And calmly knelt by his bed to pray.
He was ill and weak and decrepit too,
And this was all the old man could do.

And as he pleaded the Saviour's Word,
A double knock on the door was heard,
And his wife cried out from the old crock's rim;
"A letter, Frankey, from our boy Tim!"

Then they broke the seal with greatest care,
And an English five-pound note was there.
Said Frankey, brushing away a tear,
"God's children never starve, my dear."

The Christmas Fire

The log blazed bright on the chimney stone,
Where an old man sat in his chair alone:
No, not alone; for strange phantoms came
And danced awhile in the flickering flame;
And looks of love from faces bland
Gleamed forth from the cells of the burning brand.

He saw his brothers and sisters blest
Where the daisies smiled by the skylark's nest:
His playmates came with their cheeks of joy,
With hoop and marbles, as when a boy;
And the carol-chanters adown the moor
Were singing beside the rectory door.

And one he had loved when his youth was green
Stood out from the embers the flames between,
With a smile like spring when the sunshine glows
On the emerald slopes and the opening rose;
And the old man drew his chair still nigher,
While a tear fell down on the Christmas fire.

And then his daughters across the sea
And his sons came back to their father's knee;
And he heard their laughter among the trees,
When summer was fanning the fragrant leas;
And the prayers returned when the day was spent,
And the traveller's feet were homeward bent.

Then a vision arose in the clear fire gleams
Of a coming age of meads and streams,
When war should die on a desert shore,
And man shoot down his man no more;
When love should hold in a silken band
The peaceful dwellers of every land.

And he looked again in the embers red,
Where Merit walked with unbowed head,
And Worth was honoured among the isles,
And Truth had earned its country's smiles,
And Peace reclined in its pastoral bower
With a crown of green corn half in flower.

Still blazed the log on the chimney stone,
Where the old man sat in his chair alone:
And he heard an echo from shore to shore
That might should trample on right no more;
That the true should live, and the false expire;
And he thanked his God by the Christmas fire.

Spring Stanzas

The first dear buds are in their mossy places,
Nursed with the love of spring;
By stream and stile outbeam their shining faces,
Where woodland echoes ring.

Adown the steeps and through the solemn sedges
Where trailing tendrils twine,
Among the trees and by the hamlet-hedges,
Awaken lays divine.

Jehovah whispereth in the trembling brier,
And, song o'erflows the leas,
Whilst every blossom is a blissful lyre,
Swept by the mystic breeze.

Throughout God's earth this murmur stayeth never,
Whilst green leaves fade and fall,
By day, by night, reminding us for ever
That He is king of all.

The Last Lullaby

The mower had left the field of grain,
And the driver whistled adown the lane;
The hardy fisherman stepped ashore,
And met his boy by his own home door;
Shone over the trees the young moon's rim,
And down from the heights stole the twilight dim,
When a sound passed by me, sweetly mild,
"Lulla-by, baby! sleep, my child!"

The evening star shone o'er the lake,
And a mystic melody filled the brake;
The brooklet murmured along the dell,
Where the glow-worms glittered beside the well;
And still that young wife's last refrain
Flowed forth a-near the lattice-pane,
So softly sad, so meekly mild,
"Lulla-by, baby! sleep, my child!"

Ah! Marvel not that my soul is stirred;
My daughter's voice was the sound I heard,
Which haunts me still when the day is dim,
And the fields o'erflow with the milkmaid's hymn;
For she's gone, she is gone to the Western land,
Where the lakes are broad and the forests grand
To sing where the dark pines fringe the wild,
"Lulla-by, baby! sleep, my child!"

But God is there, where the eagle soars,
And the grand Niagara ever roars;
Where the boundless prairie strangely swells
And the red man roams through the pathless dells.
Yes, God is there; and her heart will rise
To him, when the white moon fills the skies;
And her nursery chant shall murmur mild;
"Lulla-by, baby! Sleep, my child!"

Old Robin

Old Robin was a woodman strong, as ever felled an oak,
And not a trunk in all the woods, could stand his sturdy stroke.
'Twas wondrous how the chips would fly, e'en from the hardest tree,
As oft he answered echo back,
"Peace is the text for me."

"Peace in the hut, Peace in the hall, Peace in the field and fold,
Peace where the great ships come and go, and merchants strive for gold.
Peace at the firesides of the land, where infant ringlets nod,
And prayers ascend from mothers' knees
Peace in the church of God.

Peace in the humblest cot of reed, Peace in the mansion strong,
Peace where the rustling royal robes, through gay halls sweep along,
Peace in the barque-deck fore and aft, in every factory's bound,
As far as light and love can reach,
Or living man is found.

The solemn heavens distinctly teach, that war and waste are wrong,
The moon and stars in harmony, for ever roll along:
And though the lightnings cleave the air, and thunder roars above,
They are His messengers of grace,
All winged with heavenly Love.

The green leaves whispering in the wood, the soft winds summer-shod,
The river in its winding course, proclaim the truth of God:–
That slaughter is the sap of sin, from death's forbidden tree,
Which none pursue who follow Christ,
Peace is the text for me.

Absalom Wait

"Will nobody own thee?" said Absalom Wait
To a poor limping watch-dog just outside the gate,
All matted with mud from his paws to his crown,
With his eyelids and ears and his tail hanging down.

And he looked like a dog as the north wind blew bleak,
Who had scarcely a bone or a meal for a week.
So he patted him kindly, with musical tone,
And gave him his supper, and made him his own.

And how fond grew the watch-dog of Absalom Wait!
He would lie at his feet by the side of the grate,
He would follow his eye, would obey his command,
And was up on his legs at the beck of his hand.

He once lost his way in the midst of the moor;
His dog led him home to the step of his door.
True kindness will ever true kindness create,
And the dog saved the life of Absalom Wait.

Alice Waymont

Do you know Alice Waymont who lives up the glen?
She keeps a pet goat in a very small pen,
Which follows the spinster to market and shop,
Well-pleased at the corners the herbage to crop.

It will run at her call with a bound and a bleat,
And when she is knitting will lie at her feet;
And seems very happy to have her in sight,
And will oft at her door lick her hand with delight.

'Twas given to Alice a kid on the Carn,
For its mother had died through the fall of a barn;
So she nursed it with care at the head of the creek,
And now she is milking it all through the week.

How lovely is kindness in whatever clan,
In the beasts of the field or the bosom of man;
How it glows with the beauty of angels above,
And links the great world in a cable of love.

God Made the Birds

The green hayfields waved in the breezes of June,
And the cuckoo had paused in the midst of his tune,
When a boy softly sang where the beacon was rude,
"Twas God made the birds and the beautiful brood."

"I saw them today at the foot of the tree,
And by their sweet chirpings they murmured to me,
As I mused by the moss in delectable mood,
Twas God made the birds and the beautiful brood."

"I gladly obey the true voice in my breast;
I would not, I could not, take young from the nest,
Or eggs with the love-lines of beauty imbued,
For God made the birds and the beautiful brood."

"A nest in the bushes, or by the field sod,
Is enough to convince me that there is a God.
He speaks to my heart where no footsteps intrude
That God made the birds and the beautiful brood."

"What sorrow it causes the nest to destroy!
And I'll never give pain whilst I can give joy.
He provides me with clothes and provides me with food,
And 't was God made the birds and the beautiful brood."

The Bluebell

When the hedgerow primrose dieth,
And the brooklet wanes,
When the gentle south wind sigheth,
Then the Bluebell reigns.

O'er their heads the swallow flitteth,
In the quivering light,
Where the musing May-queen sitteth
'neath the hawthorn white.

How the odorous lowland shineth
Like a garden bower,
Where the lily-nymph reclineth
By the ruined tower!

Waves of blue roll down the mountain,
Swell along the lea;
Waves of blue beside the fountain,
Where the bright maids be.

Waves of blue upon the hedges,
By the zephyr led;
Waves of blue press by the ledges,
Waves of blue o'erhead.

Waves of blue at every bending
Down the village way,
Where the thatcher's song is blending,
With the linnet's lay:

Waves of blue and sounds of singing,
Cheat the lazy hours;
Whilst their fairy bells are ringing,
"'tis the time of flowers."

Man may read man's motives wrongly;
Worth is prized by few;
Oft the meek is hampered strongly;
Oft the false deemed true.

Your Evangel ceaseth never;
In the year's warm youth;
Teaching man to cherish ever,
Love, and hope, and truth.

The Bluebell, or Wild Hyacinth, is so well known that no description of this welcome spring visitor is needed here. It is found in every copse and lane of the land, filling the air with it's fragrance, and adding a charm to Nature too beautiful for words.

The Bramble

He who prays most feels mostly Nature's wonders,
The visions of the vale;
Hears the Eternal in the rolling thunders,
Or in the breezy dale.

The slenderest sapling of the mighty prairie,
The oak, the towering pine,
The shining mosses, dew-cups of the fairy,
Are gilt with Love Divine.

And hence the common Bramble of the thicket,
Which blossoms in the lane,
Or by the stile, or near the woodland wicket,
Will oft his gaze enchain.

There is no coppice-covert deep and tangled,
No glen, or glade of gloom,
No hedge, or height, with hardy heather spangled,
Where brambles do not bloom.

Its snowy flowers are emblems of the holy,
Beloved from childhood bright;
Yet oft esteemed not thus in garments lowly,
Though lovely as the light.

'Tis thus the wilds with melody are ringing,
The listening woods and ways;
And Bramble-blossoms are for ever singing,
To their Creator's praise.

Few persons are unacquainted with the common Bramble, whose white flowers, tinged with pink, decorate the hedges during July and August, and whose fruits are so pleasing to the simple tastes of childhood.

The Celandine

Bright clumps of buttercups are in the dingle,
Opening to kiss the sun;
And primroses and virgin cowslips mingle,
When April waters run.

And the dear Celandine is come to scatter
The clouds by Winter piled;
While in the trees the noisy rooks still chatter,
As if the woods were wild.

The fields are lovely with thy starry brightness,
Gone when the moon is up;
Tissuing the vales and hills with hallowed whiteness
Out by the harebell's cup.

Nothing is vain in ravine or by river
By fountain or by flood;
All is the bounty of the gracious Giver
For man's especial good.

And so, dear Celandine, a cheerful greeting
I fain would offer thee,
While hope and joy and youthful love are meeting,
Where Nature's songs are free.

From March till the end of May the Celandine gleams among the grass of the meadow, studding every hedge-bank with stars of gold. It is one of the gayest of our spring flowers; though it is a true lover of the sunshine, opening only on bright days. It is said to close its flowers from five o-clock in the evening until nine on the following morning.

The Daisy

A clamour on the cold highway
And through the haunts of life;
So let me once more turn away
From scenes of noise and strife,
To walk where waters murmur low
Amid the violets blue,
Where many tender wildings grow,
To muse awhile with you.

Thou shinest on the mountain-side,
And in the valley deep;
Upon the mystic moorland wide,
And by the dungeon-keep,
High o'er the ponderous prison-bar,
But half revealed to sight,
Outbeaming like a lovely star
Within the blue of night.

In garden plots thou hast thy home,
Where gorgeous flowers are piled,
And where the pilgrim's footsteps roam
On boundaries weird and wild,
To sun and rain for ever true,
Or by the brooklet's wave,
Or underneath the solemn yew
Upon the maiden's grave.

On boulder ridges rent and bare
Or by the meadow streams,
O everywhere, O everywhere
The darling Daisy gleams:
In heat, in cold, when days are drear,
When skies are black or bright,
Charming the musing eye and ear
With lessons of delight.

The hues are painted by His hand
Who flung the rainbow's form,
Begirt with many a glittering band,
Athwart the driving storm.
In every line His love is seen,
In every shade His power;
Thy Maker shineth in thy mien,
Dear little Daisy flower.

No flower is better known than the Daisy. It belongs to all times and all places, -- in the garden, in the meadow, on the grave. It is the delight of childhood and the pleasure of age, and one of God's fairest, freest gifts to mankind.

The Cowslip

I have a holier sympathy with winds and waters,
With the still glade and glen,
With flowers and blossoms, Nature's darling daughters,
Than with my fellow-men.

Hence when the Cowslip of the meadow cometh
Upon the southern lea,
And in the sun the toiling ploughboy hummeth,
I hasten forth to see.

On the low fence the gay stone-chat rejoices;
Young leaves glow in the light;
And through the dells a hundred happy voices
Are pouring forth delight.

Ye hang your yellow heads in modest meekness
From morn till shut of day,
With loving lessons of all human weakness
Passing your lives away.

And thus ye answer from benign creation,
Earth-bending and sincere;
Asserting sweetly your Divine relation
To all things lovely here.

The Cowslip blossoms in our meadows during April and May. When fully blown, it hangs its head to the earth, as if in humility. It is a source of much delight to children, who make the flowers into balls. The Cowslip-gatherer is a familiar name.

The Eyebright

How profuse are Nature's wonders!
Down where foaming water thunders,
In where shady woods are quiet,
Out where boisterous billows riot,
Up where wild winds toss and tumble,
Forth where rolling cataracts rumble;
Back where boulders bind the bushland,
Forth where lichens line the rushland;
Here where glow-worms shine and glitter,
In the lanes where linnets twitter,
On the heights and in the hollows,
Where the wakeful echo follows;
In the fields and by the fountain,
Down the moorland, up the mountain;
By the by-ways, dykes and ditches;
Out where wave the Hazel switches,
Where the golden furze-bloom blazes,
Where are ranked the snowy daisies;
Where the lambkins dance and amble;
Where the angler loves to ramble;
Everywhere Divinely showing
Nature's wonders, glory-glowing.
Thus the Eyebright pale and lowly
On the cliff-side groweth slowly,
Studs the short grass of the mountain,
Blossoms by the silver fountain,
Gives its glow to districts stalky,
Shows its green in regions chalky;
And bedecks the land with wonder
Down where foaming waters thunder.

Few who love flowers would look upon the pretty little Eyebright without intense gratification. Its pale lilac blossoms are sprinkled over the sides of the chalky cliffs, studding the short grass of the mountain, and hiding among the herbage of the pasture land. It is sometimes no more than an inch in height, and flowers from June to August.

Forget-Me-Not

There are tall wildings of the glen abiding
A-near thee neath the spray,
So that full often thou thy face art hiding
Amid their colours gay.

And yet no name or look or line is sweeter,
No flower in fairy grot
For youthful bride or queenly hand is meeter,
Than the Forget-Me-Not.

How beautiful thy simple modest blushes
Where the clear waters shine,
Murmuring their way among the emerald bushes
In many a silver line!

The eye of man is often won by coarseness
By tinsel's false degree,
By noisy cymbals cracked with utter hoarseness,
Whilst merit lies like thee.

So let me call thee my especial treasure,
Dear emblem of my lot!
Bringing to man thy share of simple pleasure,
Lowly Forget-Me-Not.

This beautifully bright blue flower is a universal favourite, and when once looked upon, is not easily forgotten. During the summer months the Forget-me-not is very common in our humid meadows, bogs, banks of rivers, rivulets and ditches. There are eight native species of the genus, and all have blue blossoms.

The Heather

God's gifts are free; the breeze that fills the dingle,
And fans the fragrant bower;
The sea-waves breaking on the shining shingle,
The light, the moss-bank flower;

The river rushing to the restless ocean,
The blue expanse above,
The forest murmurs through the pine trees' motion,
The daisy's look of love.

Last eve I met a little cottage maiden,
In weeds of linen dressed,
With white May-buds and humble hedge-flowers laden;
And, O, she looked so blest!

And days of old were round me thickly thronging;
My youth was with me still,
When I beheld with all a lover's longing
The Heather of the hill.

And still it fills me with a holy feeling,
Like some old poet's strain
Through the dim twilight of my memory stealing,
Or sounds of April rain.

There are five species of Heather, all of which may be found on the moors of Cornwall.

It affords much honey to the bees, which they extract from the little bell-flowers; and it greatly adds to the beauty of the barren hills. One tall beautiful specimen grows abundantly in the neighbourhood of the Lizard.

The Honeysuckle

Odorous climber of the wildwood,
With thy breath of balm!
Let me, as a singing child should,
Greet thee with a psalm:

In the meadow, on the moorland,
By the bog of peat,
Scenting all the sandy shoreland
From thy urns of sweet;

Loved by matron, man, and maiden,
With a free goodwill;
And the old and heavy-laden,
Creeping down the Hill.

On the hedges of the highway
Where the carriage glides;
In the narrow bending byeway,
Up the castle's sides;

Twining in the robe of summer
With the rose's leaf;
Bright with many a fair new comer,
Dear to child and chief.

Reigning on the royal ruin,
Thou art quite a queen;
O'er the hill-side odours strewing,
And the coppice green.

Thus the Honeysuckle bringeth
Nectar to the breeze,
Where true poetry ever ringeth
In the trembling trees;

Failing in thy mission never,
True to Nature's sign,
Teaching man to trust for ever
In the Power divine.

No flower delights us more than the Honeysuckle. During the whole of summer its fragrant blossoms wave about the bushes, crags and ruins of every part of our island, making the lanes lovely. When the flowers disappear, clusters of dark red berries take their places, beautifying the Autumn.

Lily of the Valley

Sweet the echo ringeth,
Lily of the Vale,
As it slowly springeth
In the woody dale,
Fairer than a princess in a maiden's tale.

Wave the trees above it,
Like the sound of strings;
All the breezes love it,
Where the throstle sings,
Kissing off it's odours with their
silver wings.

Where the wood-dove hummeth
By the waterfall,
There the Lily cometh,
Like a seraph's call,
With a tale for summer and a love for all.

Blooming by the angle
Where the waters run,
And the stonecrops spangle
Many a crevice dun,
How it loves the shadow as it loves
the sun!

Evermore it lendeth
Beauty to the scene,
Whilst to earth it bendeth
In its bower of green,
Teaching man how fatal on himself
to lean.

Sorrow loves the Lily,
Pensiveness and woe,
In the covert stilly,
Where the runnels flow,
And the twilight glimmers through
the woodbine low.

In the morn's full glory,
In the evening's calm,
It has still the story
Of a higher balm,
Of a sweeter fragrance, of a
loftier psalm.

Sweetest thoughts are blending
With it's snowy bells,
Bright with blossoms bending
Over Eden wells,
When the angels mingle in the
golden dells.

One thought, like the morning,
Makes all others pale;
Bright with truth's adorning,
Which we joy to hail;
CHRIST is called for ever Lily of the
Vale.

The very name of the sweet Lily of the Valley is pleasant to mention. It is the flower of the woods, and the daughter of May; chiefly flourishing in shady and moist places. Its leaves spring from the root, and berries succeed the bells. No flower is more prized.

The Periwinkle

In a corner moist and shady,
Where the willows grew,
And comes forth the lord and lady
With the sun and dew,
Climb the velvet Periwinkles
In their robes of blue.

Forth they look where moss is tender,
And the grass-blades low,
While the sun hides half his splendour,
When the great winds blow,
And the blue-bell and the primrose
Their dear faces show.

Stars ye shine amid the ruin
Where dead feet have trod;
Stars ye are, the rill-side strewing,
Stars on burial sod;
Stars where valley ferns are shaking,
And the hill pines nod:

Ever clinging, ever shining,
In your lowly sphere;
To a stronger closely twining
With a clasp sincere.
So would we lean on the Master,
Till life's latest year.

The rich blue flower and glossy green leaves of the Periwinkle are very beautiful. It is found in woods where the ground is moist, though we can hardly call it a common flower. The stem is trailing and the wood tough. It blossoms during May and June.

The Ragged Robin

The sound of song is in my ears for ever,
Divinely understood,
At eve and morn, low-toned, unmurmuring never,
Like music in the wood.

Hence I converse with flowers where water falleth
In sweetness down the hills,
And the quaint cuckoo to the titlark calleth,
Which follows where she wills.

The very children love the Ragged Robin,
Which to the ruin clings,
When sunshine streameth, or the breeze comes sobbing
With rain-drops on its wings.

In the farm-lane, out mid the moorland bramble,
Up on the craggy ground,
Where rabbits play, and dainty fairies ramble,
Its crimson crest is found.

Cheering the soul of man with simple beauty
From Nature's low estate,
Whose highest honour and sublimest duty
Is to submit and wait.

The Ragged Robin grows abundantly in moist meadows, and on the hedges; and rises above the grass so as to be conspicuous. It blooms by the latter end of May and during June; and the rose coloured petals are so deeply jagged as to have quite a ragged appearance. We have four native species.

The Silver Weed

Hail, my little Silver Weed!
Growing on the upland mead,
Holding out thy yellow flowers
In the roadside's broken bowers,
Blooming on the brooklet's bank
Mid the mosses smooth and dank,
And along the lone highway
Where the swallows sport and play,
And the ivy climbs the tree;
I will sing for love of thee.
Country children know thee well;
For thy roots they search the dell,
Which they roast and eat with joy,
Many a girl and many a boy.
Matron meek and maiden young,
Age with wisdom on his tongue,
Those who follow, those who lead,
Love the darling Silver Weed.
Thus when swallows skim the mere,
In the summer of the year,
And the sunshine hangs its beams
O'er the channels of the streams,
Let me tune my simple reed
To the shining Silver Weed.

The Silver Weed is very common by roadsides and on moist meadows. Its leaves are very numerous and covered with silky hairs. They have a silvery hue, and may be seen during the greater part of the year. The flowers are yellow, soft like velvet, and appear in June and July.

The Snowdrop

Queen frost is out, and through the northern doors
King Cold comes clad in snow;
The wind rolls raging down the ragged moors,
And fills the vales below.

A pure white Snowdrop smiles beneath two trees,
Whose limbs are weird and bare;
Like love, with tearful face and trembling knees,
Watching the couch of care.

My friendship wanes not for thee and thy race;
Each wilding of the glen
Brings beams of gladness to my pensive face,
More than the praise of men.

How fair thy robes, how beautiful thy form,
As here thou bendest low,
The watching angel of the wintry storm,
Which o'er the waste doth blow!

By bitter tempest beaten? So am I,
Over life's toilsome wold,
Dreaming of lands where fragrant lilies lie,
Unblighted by the cold.

The lovely white Snowdrop needs no description, it is found in woods, old orchards, and rustic places. It not unfrequently looks up out of the snow, and is hailed with delight, as the harbinger of spring. The tender little flower is evermore bent to the earth, and is greatly cultivated in gardens.

The Sweet Brier

Our years pass on like swift feet through the gloaming,
Yet earth remains the same;
The poet rambles where the rills are roaming,
The heights yield loud acclaim.

In wild rose lanes, where bud-zoned fancy pleasures,
And oft in youth we strayed,
The mother walks with her dear household treasures,
The lover with his maid.

The joy of childhood o'er the fields is ringing;
The harvest whitens still;
The belfry bells are in the ivy swinging;
The full moon tips the hill.

Sweet whispers tremble, where the moss scarce hideth
The glow-worms lamp of fire,
Filling the hollows, as the runnel glideth
On by the fragrant Brier.

Old age comes swifter than we dare believe it,
With snow-marks on the ground,
Till in the dusk we prayerfully perceive it,
And yet the world goes round.

The Sweet Brier Rose, the beauty of the lanes and woods in summer, may easily be recognised at once from all others by its sweetly scented leaves. It is a great favourite with young and old, and is supposed to be the "eglantine" of ancient writers

The Wild Rose

I cannot tell how it may be with others
Over life's sandy plain,
But I have loved the hedges as my brothers
In summer and in rain.

And still I go to them in hours of weakness,
When overcome with fears,
Weighed down with sorrow, and beset with bleakness,
To weep away my tears.

But oftener do I seek their silent arches,
As some bright vision glows,
Cheered with the whisper of the solemn larches
And the red-rimmed Wild Rose.

It shines among the filberts sun-surrounded,
Smiles in the brambles drear,
Outpours its sweets where dryness long abounded
The beauty of the year.

Sad eyes turn to it, and they gleam for gladness;
Care half-forgets its woes;
It has a charm for much of human sadness
The beautiful Wild Rose.

In the rich hedges there is not in summer a lovelier flower than the Wild Rose, of which we have eighteen species. The Rose is rightly called "the queen of flowers" and is the favourite of all lands. The hips, which succeed the flowers, form a valuable store of food for birds.

The Wood Anemone

In the hollows of the moor,
By the timid rabbit's door,
Down the dells where quiet reigns,
Up the hillocks, out on plains
Where the velvet moss-cups be,
Shines the Wood Anemone.

In thy May-bower sweet with song
Gleamest thou the whole day long,
Where the welcome blue-bells glow,
And the violets bending low,
While thy harpist is the bee,
Little Wood Anemone!

Thus thou dwellest on the down,
Where the Druid won renown,
Who perchance beheld in thee
An eternal mystery,
Whispering by the alter-stone
Of the wonderful Unknown.

Let me, to thy footstool sent,
Learn the lessons of content,
Striving ever in my sphere
To be honest and sincere;
Not in great things to excel,
But to do my little well.

No flower of spring is more beautiful than the Wood Anemone. It grows in woods, on mountains and in sheltered valleys. There are four species, varying in colour, but all silky and beautiful. They are found abundantly near the castle on Carn Brea Hill.

My First Essay

THERE is a certain circle in which the beasts of the forest, the birds of the air, and the fishes of the sea have been revolving from the time when the Ark rested on the top of Mount Ararat down to the present generation. The swallow comes and goes in its season. It floats over the lakes and rivers, glides up the hillside and down into the valley, feeds upon the wing, and builds its nest in the same manner as it did centuries ago.

The cow grazes among the daisies, drinks at the running brook, and yields her milk under the hawthorn in precisely the same way as she did when our grandmothers were alive. The fish inhabit the rivers and lakes, and gambol in the ocean, as they have ever been wont. They have never passed over the circle.

But man has been advancing in intellect age after age. He has reined the elements to his iron chariot, hurrying it over the exalted valleys and levelled hills. He has chiselled his way into the mineralled earth, until its discovered treasures magnify the comforts of man, and fill the hearts of myriads with gladness. He has soared into the firmament, until the beautiful earth has dwindled into a speck, and the leaping, quivering lightning has been tamed in his grasp. He has stretched the word-breathing wire over continent and sea, and now the ends of the world meet in a grand hymn of joy.

The hill-slopes reached by our ancestors are left far behind by the present generation, and untrodden heights are now attained at which they feared to gaze. How little did they know of reading or writing, – those sublime sorcerers which in the present day hold the great world in thrall! Think of them, when able to express themselves in signs and characters similar to the letters of our alphabet, writing upon the bark of trees and square blocks of wood. Now we have paper of the finest quality; And books full of good men's thoughts woo us on the shelves of the peasant and the peer.

Now a Bible may be procured for a less number of pence than it used to cost pounds. How few of our forefathers could read, even a century ago, whose descendants of eight years old repeat large portions of the Holy scriptures from memory! Man is stepping over the circle. Shakespeare, Milton, and Newton have lived. What the world shall be remains for us to do. Education must take its proper place in our land. The young must be instructed in higher and holier things; and higher and holier things must be taught to their progeny, till the golden fruit of the grand millennium fill the whole earth.

When the Sun

When the sun creates another day, we two are one,
Blent like the light and rose leaves. Blessed hour!
I seem to bathe in nectar, and the waves
Come murmuring round me more delicious still,
A preface to my volume of delight.
Now let me lead thee homeward at a slow pace,
Loitering at every turn, as lovers will,
Creating seraphs out of every leaf,
And theme for dalliance from the softest sound.
Thus we depart with kisses.

Home

O! when at last I'm sleeping in the grave
Where the wild flowerets whisper o'er my head,
And the soft breezes chime my mournful dirge
At vesper time – O! if an Angel's wing
May stoop to brush the dew-drop from the flowers,
And visit scenes it loved – then I'll descend,
Swiftly descend, beneath the purple eve,
Fanning the heath-bush with my pinions bright,
And hover o'er this loveliest spot of all!

The Hilltop

But here I am, with heaven above my head,
O'er run with beauty, and great thoughts like ships
Gliding across the waters of my soul;
The earth below me like a teeming mart.
So renovated, so refreshed am I,
If I had wings I'd flash into the air,
And strive with all the marvel of a sage
To grasp this growing grandeur. In the woods
At summer twilight, I have heard strange songs
Travelling among the shadows, and my strength
Grew as the notes waxed louder, till I felt
The sinews of a giant, and strode on
With supple limbs through seas of solemn sound,
Feeling no weariness, forgetting pain
And followed by an angel. But this height
Brings organ swells, and crash of lifted trumps,
And sounding odes from choirs whose wings are flame,
Whose harps are moulded in the fires of love,
That I grow big with blessing.

Essay IV

A Ramble to Mylor Churchyard

MYLOR churchyard is near Falmouth, Cornwall and is well worthy of a visit by all those who delight in nature and quietude. Almost surrounded by the sea, the deep music of whose waters is rolling there for ever-more, it is a fit sleeping-place for the bold mariners, many of whom lie under its green sward, and the margin of their graves is almost kissed by the murmuring main. Far away from the din and tumult of town or city, it woos the lover of meditation to its paths of peace and at all times and at all seasons, whether Spring calls forth the shining buds, or Summer reposes in her bower of leaves, or Autumn smiles by the corn-sheaf, or Winter spreads its snow garments over the hills. I have seen it under almost all those different aspects, and beauty has always been its dower.

My friends and I had been standing by the brink of a beautiful river, on a calm August evening, watching the happy harvesters returning from the fields, and musing on Capern's all-glorious harvest hymn, beginning, –

"God bless you, merry harvesters! Down with the golden grain!
I love to hear your sickle-strokes enlivening the plain."

We then started off on our intended ramble, crossed the ferry for Flushing, and away by the old tree, up the hill through the wood, over the stubble-meadows and grassy leas, away and away in the dusky twilight to the quaint old churchyard of Mylor. The sun had long set, the stars were looking lovingly down upon the quiet earth, the chime of the evening bells came floating over the waters, strangely recalling the musical words of Moore, –

"Those evening bells, those evening bells,
How many a tale their music tells,
Of youth and home, and that sweet time
When first I heard their soothing chime!"

The bat crept out of its hiding place, and was wheeling by with a pleasant "whirr;" the harvester was sitting in his home, after the labours of the day, blessing the great Father for the bounties of His providence; silence crept over the hollows, and nought was heard but the dip of the oar of the boatman in the shining waters of the river, which slept at our feet like a sheet of crystal, as we wound our way down the sloping meads, on by the sea-side, and then over the rural stile into the tree-covered churchyard.

And such a solemn place, at such a solemn hour! The darkness was made more palpable here by the shadows of the old trees, which cloaked us in their shrouds like the skirts of the god of gloom. We all involuntarily uncovered our heads from pure reverence, and glided among the graves like so many disembodied spirits, not uttering a word. Tombs stood thick on the uneven sward, of almost every form and every fashion and seemed as if they were strangely watching our movements in the gathering darkness and wondering at the deep silence of our course.

One old yew tree, near the sea-side entrance, is remarkably large; I never saw such a noble specimen before in any "City of the dead." It spreads its mighty branches far around, which cannot be much less than sixty feet in diameter. We were sorry to learn from a courteous inhabitant of this favoured spot, that some selfish individuals have recently been lopping off its giant limbs and turning them into pieces of household furniture, more careful to fill their purses than preserve this sacred relic of the olden times. O, shame upon their sacrilegious hands! Could our voice be heard amid the rush of those earnest seekers after gain, we would utter a piercing cry, "O, spare the old yew tree."

Under its far spreading branches, in a deep wide grave, lie a heap of human beings, who were drowned at the loss of the "Transport" on Trefusis Point many years ago. The yew is, however, grand and solemn, and awe-inspiring enough in itself; and I could not gaze on it without recalling Tennyson's fine words, –

> "Old yew, which graspest at the stones
> That name the under-lying dead,
> Thy fibres net the dreamless dead;
> Thy roots are wrapt about the bones

> "The seasons bring the flower again,
> And bring the firstling to the flock,
> And in the dusk of these, the clock
> Beats out the little lives of men.

> "O, not for thee the glow, the bloom,
> Who changest not in any gale;
> Nor branding summer suns avail
> To touch thy thousand years of gloom."

The small Gothic church, which is supposed to be eight or nine hundred years old, stands almost in the centre of the churchyard, and nothing was lacking at that solemn hour to clothe it with traditionary romance. Thick, green ivy clambered up by the door, hung over the low eaves as if watching the slumbering dead, and pierced in at the fretted windows.

Gray's Elegy written in a Country Churchyard came back upon our memories, and its deep-toned melodies were sounding through our souls. We approached the old ivy-covered belfry, which is a living poem of itself, and stood on one of the green hillocks. Not a leaf was stirring. Nature seemed breathless with awe. Not a sound broke upon the ear, save when ever and anon a sportive wavelet rolled up from the river, almost laving the green sod of some quiet sleeper.

Suddenly we held our breath, and gazed wonderingly at each other; for even as this solemn silence was possessing our very souls, and bringing them into fit sympathy with the hour and the place, a hoarse weird tone saluted our ears, similar to the snore of some weary dreamer after the fatigues of a days toil. We looked up at the little tower whence the sound came, but could see nothing. It must have been the song of the night owl cheering his mate.

We had lingered so long in the meditative silence, that we were too late for the ferry, and so had to hire a boat to take us to the quay. As we were silently gliding over the still harbour, the moon suddenly rose from behind a hill, shedding her welcome beams upon the waters, and we seemed paddling through a lake of silver. We had stars below and stars above, ships at anchor and ships afloat, sheets of lurid light in the blue deep, as well as in the smoky town; and over all hung pale Cynthia like an angel shedding mystic peace around.

Joy was in our hearts, as we marked and treasured up for future delight all the pictures of loveliness and beauty which were so profusely scattered around us; and we returned to our home that night with a feeling that we had never known before that the earth was so beautiful.

The Village Lane

O'ershadow'd, still retreat,
Track trod by tuneful feet,
Haunt of the swallow, robin's
rich domain,
The freehold of the wren,
The fairies chamber when
The moon is fullest!
Welcome, village lane.

Beneath some ancient trees,
Shook by the sighing breeze,
A few roods past the last house
and the mill,
Bubbles the village well,
Where lads and lasses tell
The hamlet's wonders
when the day is still.

Yes, here true lovers stray,
When comes the cool of day,
Whispering their loves beneath the
hawthorn tree,
Forgetful how the night
Steals o'er the darkening height,
And living each
that each might happier be.

And who, though earthly poor,
Begrimed with care all o'er,
And sadly sad as ever sad can be,
Would not forget his pain
When lingering down the lane,
Where robin builds
within the hollow tree?

How sweet to wander here,
When vespers murmur clear,
Tuning my harp betwixt the
day and night!
Then pictures, fairer far
Than sky or peering star,
Throng on my vision
o'er the dusky height.

At such a quiet hour
There comes a soothing power,
Found only in the path of solitude;
And voices in the breeze,
And voices in the trees,
Are richly laden
with the spirit's food.

Why crowd the sickly street,
With noisy, feverish heat,
Where not a bud or living leaf is seen,
But hills of brick and stone,
Where weary wretches groan,
When you may wander
where the walls are green?

Come to the village lane,
Enjoy its calm again,
As Eve steals forth to bead her
favourite flower;
Beneath the woodbine sit,
Where bats in silence flit,
And muse on life
beyond earth's little hour.

Winter

Old Winter is come, spreading ice on the moor,
And wailing like woe at the cottager's door.
He has blighted the heather that bloom'd on the hill,
Stalk'd down in the valley and glass'd o'er the rill,
Sipp'd up the clear pools with their moss-cover'd brim,
And placed his cold hand on the daisy's white rim.
Old Winter, old Winter, come, hie thee away,
And let the soft breeze with the daffodils play.

O look on the trees! they are leafless and bare;
Not a bud, not a blossom, of beauty is there.
Hoarse wails through the branches eternally go,
And the cot in the valley is cover'd with snow;
While down from the eaves hang the icicles cold,
And Cock Robin mourns on the sleety threshold.
Old Winter, old Winter, come, hie thee away,
And let the sunbeams with the gossamer play.

But, ah! it is vain to invoke him to go;
For the crest of the hill is a cold wreath of snow.
Wherever I look, 't is the same to my sight,
Mead, mountain, and moorland are mantled in white;
In his palace of ice, at the back of a rock,
He moans that the crag-heaps seem rent with the shock.
Old Winter, old Winter, O leave our dear land,
And revel where ice-hills eternally stand.

The grey-headed man, clad in rags as he goes,
And the water-cress girl, with the frost in her toes,
I saw them to-day creeping down the dark lane,
And they trembled with cold, and were weeping with pain.
Thou hast but a season, old Winter, to roar,
And then I know surely thy reign will be o'er,
And thou must be off to the frost-bitten zone,
And beautiful Spring have thy septre and throne.

Before reading on, the following report may be of interest:–

"Mr Harris is known to us. His gold has already been stamped as of true ring at the mint of public opinion, and the volume before us contains some well and carefully written essays, in addition to the musical outpourings of the poets heart. The volume opens with a few glimpses of the poet's early life, and shows that though he may not have been –

> 'Cradled into poetry by wrong,
> And learn'd in suffering what he taught in song,'

He must have felt the world cold, hard, and callous, as he grew up, comparatively neglected, to a life of toil, which is embodied in the 'Story of Carn Brea,' and which extends over several books. We may instance the 'Hartley Hero,' as an instance of how fearful mining calamities are regarded by those who daily dig in the bowels of the earth. We shall no doubt, meet Mr. Harris again ere long, and in the mean time we cordially recommend the volume to all who are not fond of true poetry, but who feel a delight in encouraging talent wherever it may be found."

– The Royal Leamington Spa Courier and Warwickshire Standard,
April 29th, 1865.

The Hartley Hero

Morn came, and night departed,
    Although it linger'd late,
And on the eaves the sparrow
    Was calling to his mate;
When from his couch the miner
    Arose and kiss'd his boy,
And sought again his coal-cave,
    And dangerous employ.

He carols down the footpath,
    And leaps the village stile,
Thinking upon his baby
    And wife and home the while.
He dashes off the tear-drop
    That steals into his eye,
And turns to see his dwelling,
    Though scarcely conscious why.

Alas, alas, poor miner,
    Thou 'lt never see it more,
Or hear thy baby's footfall
    Upon the cottage floor!
Even now the dark death-angel
    On dismal wing hath sped,
And in the grey of morning
    Is hovering o'er thy head.

Soon down into the darkness
    With song does he descend,
To toil with the two hundred
    Whose lives so soon will end.
Sing, mother, to thy darling
    A sad and solemn strain;
Thy husband and its father
    Will ne'er come back again.

A crash was heard, so sudden,
It seem'd a bolt from heaven,
And soon it was discover'd
The engine-bob was riven.
Half fell within the building,
Half in the shaft was hurl'd,
Filling the only passage
Up from the under-world.

Amid the falling rubbish,
And timbers cracking round,
And groans of dying workmen,
A praying prince is found.
And one hand grasps the promise
The Bible truths afford,
And one the robe of Jesus,
The ever-living Lord.

He risk'd his life for others,
Who trembled near the goal,
If he could save their bodies,
Or cheer the parting soul.
O hero, noble hero,
Not shedding human blood,
But walking in the footsteps
Of thy Reedemer God.

The song of after ages
Thy story shall rehearse,
And harps not yet enkindled
Embalm thy deed in verse;
And glory, fairer, brighter
Than ever warrior won,
Shall stream upon thy pathway,
And gild life's setting sun.

O harp, pour tones of sorrow
Upon the heavy air!
Four, five, six days departed,
And still those men were there.
O hundreds – sons, and fathers,
And brothers, in the gloom,
The gas, and greedy blackness,
Which proved a living tomb.

Not one escaped to tell us
What cries and prayers were made,
How son embraced his father
Within this dreadful shade;
Or brother cheer'd his brother,
And bade him look on high,
And trust his soul to Jesus,
As death came stealing by.

All perish'd. What a number
Of England's noble sons,
Her strength, her hope, her riches,
Her true heroic ones!
When by the fire we cluster,
As day's pale beams depart,
We'll think upon the miner,
And take him to our heart.

O Saviour, save the widow,
With grief and care oppress'd,
And winter on her spirit;
O take her to Thy breast.
Shine through this dispensation,
Thou who for all hast bled;
Uphold the sinking mother,
And give the orphan bread.

O 'tis a fearful story,
We tremble at the sound;
And hope in cruel darkness
They mercy sought and found.
O Hartley, scene of mourning
And desolation deep!
For evermore shall Sorrow
And Pity o'er thee weep

Not Yet

The twilight was departing,
The bee had found his hoard,
The bard was at his jingle,
The lamp upon the board;
When Alfred's eyes grew heavy,
As if about to close,
Where dreams are gilt with summer,
And song eternal flows.

His mother kiss'd his forehead,
And smooth'd his shining hair;
"Come, go to bed, my darling,
And sleep so sweetly there.
I'll watch you by the window,
Beside my mignonette."
"No, no," said little Alfred,
"No, mother dear, not yet."

And as his sweet lips falter'd
The burden of his mind,
Said I, This is an emblem
Of much of human kind:
Amid life's endless struggle,
With care and pain beset,
Respecting what is rightful
The answer is, "Not yet."

"Not yet," replies the sluggard,
As, sitting in his shed,
The summer breeze is sighing
Across his thistle bed.
His rags become more ragged,
His garden wilder grows,
His frame and fences thinner,
Till hunger ends his woes.

"Not yet," replies the drunkard,
When conscience plies him sore,
And urges him to duty,
And bids him sin no more.

"Not yet; another revel,
Till crowing of the cock;"
And down the fearful vortex
He rushes like a rock.

"Not yet," replies the swearer,
When, at the close of day,
His sins start up before him,
In all their black array.
"Not yet; I may to-morrow;"
And in his storm of strife
Is hurl'd the shaft of judgment,
And ends his wretched life.

"Not yet," replies the liar;
"One morsel more, forsooth,
Beneath my tongue delicious,
And then I'll speak the truth."
And as he framed the falsehood
Within his harden'd heart,
Death rush'd upon him quickly,
And slew him with his dart.

"Not yet," replied the schoolboy,
As on his way he ran:
"I'll give my heart to Jesus
When in the weeds of man."
Time pass'd, his soul grew harder;
Age came, his locks were thin;
"Not yet, not yet," he shouted,
Until he died in sin.

And thus it is in error,
In foolishness and pride,
Too oft the wrong is cherish'd
And right is thrust aside.
O labour rightly, promptly,
Before life's sun is set,
And hurry off for ever
The fatal words, "Not yet."

The Burial

Will's ferret was buried this morn:
When Samuel came down from his bed,
He whisper'd, with aspect forlorn,
"O, Kitty, Will's ferret is dead."

And Kitty soon told it to Mark,
And Mark to the rest of his clan.
We sorrow'd with visages dark,
As if we were mourning a man.

"Come, Ann, let us lay her to rest,
And you must prepare us a bier:
We will heap the cold earth on her breast;"
And we wiped from our eyelids a tear.

So Ann made a coffin so small,
Of cast-off brown paper and thread:
This served for a shroud and a pall, –
False trappings, unknown to the dead.

And Samuel was sexton and clerk,
And Benjamin bearer so brave,
While Kitty, and Jacob, and Mark
Soon bore her away to the grave.

My mother was curious now,
And so she came softly behind,
Well pleased with her children, I trow,
Who to the poor brute were so kind.

'Neath the hawthorn its grave was dug deep,
With sharp-pointed pickaxe and spade.
Lie down, little ferret, and sleep
On the couch that affection has made.

Home

Melodious word,
Melting my colder passions into tears,
Rearing a bulwark round my shatter'd frame
And speaking joy.

Sacred to me,
Who own no mansion towering 'mid the trees,
But shelter'd in my father's hollow shed,
Straw-thatch'd,

Do oft at eve
Peer through my lattice on the rising moon,
Or gaze spell-bound on the bright western star,
Sinking to rest.

Or, stretch'd along
In the cool shadow of my cottage eaves,
Woo the sweet twilight's song, and strike
My pensive harp.

Ay, even now,
When musing in my mountain's broomy bowers,
Kiss'd with song-laden winds, I feel
"The spells of home."

My early home,
On the blue hill-top 'mid the lichen'd rocks,
Where Solitude in cells where fairies chime
Rests undisturb'd!

O spot empearl'd!
Amid thy stillness it were sweet to dwell,
With bush and towering crag; then die at last
In sight of heaven.

AN ODE

ON THE TERCENTENARY ANNIVERSARY OF

WILLIAM SHAKESPERE,

APRIL 23RD, 1864.

PRIZE POEM.

"The area of competition was unlimited, and the competitors numerous. Mr Harris has, by carrying off the Shakspere Prize, open to all, made a national reputation."

(Keene's Bath Journal, June 18th 1864)

Acknowledgements

THE Committee Members of the John Harris Society wish to thank all who assisted in making this publication possible.

The Royal Cornwall Museum, Truro, for the loan of the candle-holder, ink well and quill pen for the front cover photograph.

The front cover photograph includes an original document in the handwriting of John Harris, which was generously donated to the Society by Diane Hodnett during 2008.

The Cornish Studies Library, Redruth, for access to and copying of the Photograph of John Harris, plus various books and documents.

Kerrier District Council and The Camborne Town Council for their generous financial grants and support.

The John Harris Society also wish to thank Les Merton of Palores Publications and The St. Ives Printing & Publishing Company for their professional advice and assistance.

List of Subscribers

Name of subscriber   *copies*

Rev'd David Everett,
founder of the John Harris Society 2
Mr J. T. Andrews 2
Mr W.E. Dodge 1
Mr Stan Gore 1
Mrs Kathryn Garrod 1
Miss B. M. Hewett 1
Mr Bryan Teague 2
Mrs Eve Parsons 2
Mr Eric Parsons 2
Mrs Jo Mynott 2
Professor Charles Thomas 2
The Royal Institution of Cornwall Museum 1
Mr Tony Langford 3
Mrs Caroline Palmer 1
Mr Alex Palmer 1
Mr Stuart Cullimore 1
Mrs Helene Cullimore 1
Mr Alan Sanders 1
Mr Huw Rowe 1
Mr John Gillbard 1
Mr Bernard Gillbard 1
Mr Les Merton 1
Miss Karen Merton 1
Miss Lynn Merton 1
Miss Zena Merton 1
Mrs Elisabeth Rickard 4
Mr Paul Langford 2
Mrs Ann Trevenen-Jenkin 2
Ms Jackie Harding 2
Mr Michael Howarth 2
Mr Adrian Lake 1

Mr R. F. Cope - Walters & Barbary 1
Mrs M. Taylor 1
Miss Barbara Tripp 1
Mrs M. Burtenshaw 1
Mr John Hodge 1
Mr Bernard and Nancy Rudden 1
Mrs Marguerite Williams 1
Mrs Eleanor Bowell 1
Mr Jeff Collins 1
Margaret Penna 2
Mrs Dawn E. Williams 2
Mrs Joan Biscoe 1
Mr John Fleet 1
Julia Hitchon 4